VOLUME 12

NORTH AMERICAN
B-25 MITCHELL

By Frederick A. Johnsen

Copyright © 1997 Frederick A. Johnsen

Published by
Specialty Press Publishers and Wholesalers
11481 Kost Dam Road
North Branch, MN 55056
United States of America
(612) 583-3239

Distributed in the UK and Europe by
Airlife Publishing Ltd.
101 Longden Road
Shrewsbury
SY3 9EB
England

ISBN 0-933424-77-9

All rights reserved. No part of this book may be reproduced or transmitted in any form or by any means, electronic or mechanical including photocopying, recording or by any information storage and retrieval system, without permission from the Publisher in writing.

Material contained in this book is intended for historical and entertainment value only, and is not to be construed as usable for aircraft or component restoration, maintenance or use.

Designed by Greg Compton

Printed in the United States of America

TABLE OF CONTENTS

THE NORTH AMERICAN B-25 MITCHELL

PREFACE **4**

A WORD FROM THE AUTHOR

CHAPTER 1: TACTICAL REALITIES **5**

THE ARGUMENTS FOR THE B-25

CHAPTER 2: DESIGN AND DEVELOPMENT **16**

EACH MODEL MEETS A NEED

CHAPTER 3: ICONS OVER TOKYO **46**

DOOLITTLE RAID ASSURED B-25'S PLACE IN HISTORY

CHAPTER 4: THE B-25 GOES TO WAR **49**

USAAF MITCHELLS AROUND THE WORLD

SPECIAL FULL COLOR SECTION: A LITTLE COLOR, PLEASE **65**

B-25 PAINT AND MARKINGS

CHAPTER 5: NEW JOBS **91**

POST-WAR B-25 OPERATORS

CHAPTER 6: THE HEART OF THE MATTER **95**

CARE AND FEEDING OF THE B-25

SIGNIFICANT DATES **100**

KEY DATES IN THE HISTORY OF THE B-25 MITCHELL

Preface

A Word From the Author

Its cranked wing and angular twin tails are unmistakable. Its chugging, businesslike roar heralds its approach and telegraphs pugnacity. The North American Aviation B-25 Mitchell is, and acts like, a scrappy warrior from the word go.

No doubt part of its heroic stature derives from its namesake, the outspoken Gen. Billy Mitchell who proved once and for all that bombers could destroy targets, and that wars would nevermore be decided only on land or sea. And then another genuine hero of American stock, Jimmy Doolittle, took 16 B-25s and peopled them with brave volunteers who threw away the book and launched from an aircraft carrier to bomb Tokyo in April 1942.

Soon, B-25 crews around the world were improvising and flinging the war back to the Axis powers. USAAF Mitchell bombers skip-bombed Japanese ships at mast-top height, and formation-bombed German targets in Italy from altitude. British crews took the Mitchell to war, and Soviet bomber pilots sometimes treated the B-25 like an aerobatic airplane, to the amazement of their USAAF counterparts.

This account of North American Aviation's B-25 was enhanced by help from a variety of people and organizations, including Aero Trader (Carl Scholl and Tony Ritzman), Norm Avery, Gene Boswell (North American), Peter M. Bowers, Columbia Airmotive (Bob, Dave, and Jeff Sturges), Jeff Ethell, Albert W. James, Helen F. Johnsen, Kenneth G. Johnsen, Sharon Lea Johnsen, Don Keller, Dennis Peltier, Milo Peltzer, and numerous veterans of the 12th Bomb Group (including Alex Adair, Marv Hawkins, and Bob Wilson).

After 12th Bomb Group had been in north Africa a while, the deicer boots came off as unnecessary. RAF fin flash spanned space between middle two hinges on vertical fin. "Earthquakers" on Jeep was nickname of 12th BG; passengers were a troupe of entertainers from South Africa. (12th Bomb Group Association)

A special word is in order about the men of the 12th Bomb Group. Theirs is a strong association that supports commemorations of the unit's accomplishments and its globetrotting history, with an itinerary that stretched from McChord Field in Washington state to north Africa, and on to the China-Burma-India Theater of Operations. Decades after the end of World War Two, the men of the 12th Bomb Group Association typified those who served in and around the durable B-25 Mitchell bomber. Their enthusiasm, support, and genuine friendship are greatly appreciated.

Ray Wagner and the staff of the San Diego Aerospace Museum accommodated my photo research in their files. Photos gleaned from that source are noted by the abbreviation SDAM in the captions; other abbreviations used in this volume include USAAF for United States Army Air Forces, USAF for United States Air Force and NAA for North American Aviation.

*In Memory of
Jeffrey L. Ethell
1947-1997*

FREDERICK A. JOHNSEN
1997

TACTICAL 1 REALITIES

THE ARGUMENTS FOR THE B-25

During World War One, the French and British found strategic bombardment to be costly in lives lost and airplanes downed. But the Allies quickly grasped the utility of aircraft for interdicting enemy supply lines. By 1918, Air Service operations of the American Expeditionary Force were led by Brig. Gen. Billy Mitchell, who executed a well-planned aerial interdiction campaign in conjunction with the fighting at St. Mihiel in September. With peace, there followed a typical posture around the world to subjugate a nation's air forces under the control of the army; interdiction, after all, was to support the army in its land battles.[1]

The evolution of bombardment aviation between World War One and World War Two was a sometimes-forced amalgam of technological advances and evolving doctrine. American strategic bombardment proponents were in the ascendancy in the 1930s, realizing that the strategic arena afforded the Air Corps the venue of greatest freedom from Army control. Strategic bomber backers carefully protected and nurtured the four-engine B-17 Flying Fortress even at a time when Congress preferred to spend bomber funds on cheaper twin-

Quartering photo of NA-40B showed lines that would evolve into the B-25 Mitchell. Wing-mounted machine guns protruded from leading edges. (McElroy collection)

Chatter Box, a 90th Bomb Squadron strafer, had early-style single blister encasing both package guns. Extra skin to protect aircraft structure from muzzle blast of package guns is evident beneath nickname. (NAA)

NORTH AMERICAN B-25 MITCHELL

Mortimer, an early strafer conversion for the 90th Bomb Squadron in the Pacific, was photographed first in standard bomber configuration before modification. (NAA)

During conversion of Mortimer into a commerce destroyer, the bombsight window was removed and the resulting opening was enlarged and squared off to take .50-caliber machine guns. (NAA)

The finished commerce destroyer Mortimer, sporting four new fixed nose guns and a patch where the flexible upper nose gun had been, was photographed with NAA tech reps Jim Clemens (left) and Larry York. (NAA)

engine Douglas B-18s. Strategic bombardment advocates in the Air Corps occasionally ruffled Navy officials with proclamations and demonstrations of what airpower could do. Meanwhile, tactical bombardment stewards sometimes cast a jaundiced eye at their ground-bound Army counterparts, guarding against having tactical air assets weakened by parceling them out to ground commanders piecemeal, thereby limiting unified air operations.

Often idealistic Air Corps officers gravitated to the various philosophical camps in their service; if strategic bombing received most of the headlines, tactical bombing advocates nonetheless were able to plant the seeds of design that moved their specialty beyond the thinking of the 1930s and into the next decade with potent aircraft including the B-25.

The North American NA-40 twin engine bomber that was to evolve into the B-25 hinted at improvements over the B-18s, B-23s, and older B-10s and B-12s of the 1930s. Its use of tricycle landing gear was a first for American bombers. As evolved into the B-25, the use of a manned tail gun emplacement was

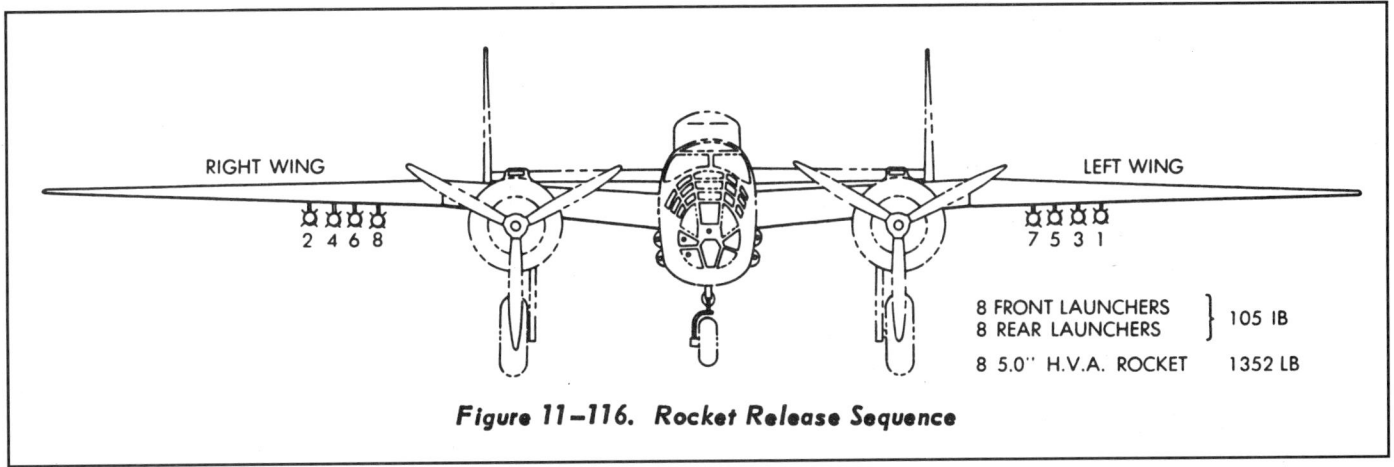

The B-25J could be fitted with eight HVARs (High Velocity Aircraft Rockets), depicted in a firing-sequence diagram. (Don Keller/Bob Sturges)

a harbinger only recently seen on the B-23. The decision to replace the NA-40's original R-1830 engines with R-2600s was another fortuitous selection that gave the B-25 the power it needed. (In an ironic repeat of this decades later, civilian operators of R-1830-powered PB4Y-2 Privateer patrol bombers opted to switch to R-2600 engine packages from B-25s.)

When western Europe reeled under German blitzkrieg warfare in the summer of 1940, American President Franklin Roosevelt espoused expansion of the Air Corps to include 54 groups, the bomber component of which was to consist of heavy B-17s and B-24s, and medium B-26s and B-25 Mitchells.[2]

It was clear not all bombers could do all things. Four-engine B-24s, with a range of 2,100 miles while carrying 5,000 pounds of bombs, could out-reach and out-deliver the B-25C, at 1,500 miles carrying 3,000 pounds of bombs.[3] But in 1942, at $153,396, a typical B-25 cost about half as much as a B-24. Small, brisk B-25s were more appropriate to use as treetop strafers than were lumbering B-17s and B-24s. Generally delineated concepts of strategic and tactical bombardment gave the heavy bombers a high-altitude perch from which to make mass attacks on targets of strategic importance, while medium bombers like the B-25 worked at medium and low altitudes to strike at a mixture of pre-ordained targets as well as impromptu targets of opportunity. To be sure, the separation of strategic and tactical bombardment occasionally blurred during World War Two, with single-ship attacks by B-25s against Japanese shipping taking on strategic significance due to Japan's reliance on a far-ranging network of shipping to bring raw materials to that country's factories.

The shorter range of medium bombers like the B-25 suggested an immediacy to their use, closer to

Rugged Desert Warrior of 12th Bomb Group returned to the United States for a morale tour, sporting a map showing its exploits in the Mediterranean, where the 12th BG fulfilled the Mitchell's promise as a tactical interdiction and close air support weapon. (12th Bomb Group Association)

Early B-25C shows unusually stark demarcation between upper and lower surface camouflage; red propeller warning band wraps around underside of forward fuselage. (SDAM)

the front, where they often delivered tactical blows to the enemy to hurt his ability to attack Allied ground forces. The four-engine heavy bombers could carry the war farther to the enemy's strategic rear areas, and this disparity in range was best accommodated by selecting targets capitalizing on the capabilities of each type of bomber.

World War Two provided the setting to evolve tactical air doctrine. In north Africa in 1942, a British model of control evolved in which strategic and tactical air assets were assigned missions by an air commander, based on requests from a ground commander, although both men reported to a ground officer who was theater commander. This had the effect of giving the air forces more control and unification over their deployment, while still giving the ground army theater commander the ultimate control. Given the chance, the air commanders were able to show their army counterparts the real value of having air assets parceled

A 1939 NAA rendering depicted a Mitchell more rounded than actual aircraft would be; gunners in waist section were shown with hand-held weapons that would be unsuitable in combat. (NAA/SDAM)

When NAA installed R-2800-51 engines, with oversized propeller spinners and redesigned cowlings, on B-25H number 43-4406, the resulting NA-98X hybrid handily outpaced a standard H-model by as much as 70 miles an hour in some conditions. After only three weeks of testing, on 24 April 1944, following a high speed pass and pull-up over

the NAA Inglewood ramp, both outer wing panels ripped off, knocking the tail off as the lone NA-98X spread a trail of wreckage in a crash fatal to both crew members, and terminating the project. (NAA/SDAM)

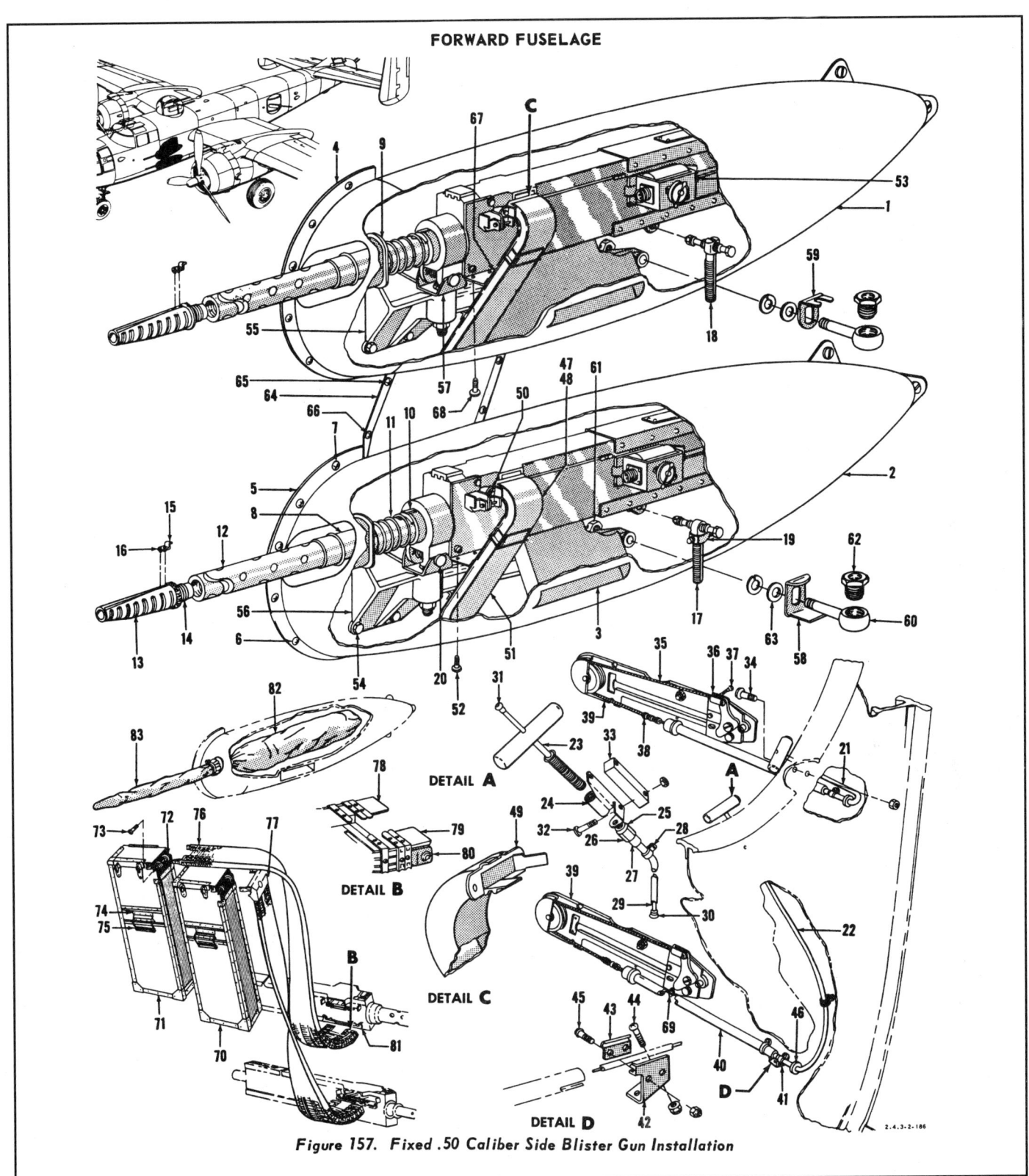

Figure 157. Fixed .50 Caliber Side Blister Gun Installation

Production blister gun packages typically were individual shapes for each gun with an angled connecting piece between them used to transport spent links from the upper gun to the lower housing, from which they dropped in flight. Tall ammo boxes inside the fuselage fed the package guns. Tapered vented blast deflectors (part number 13) were fitted to many B-25 blister gun installations to help keep blast damage to the fuselage to a minimum. (Keller/Sturges)

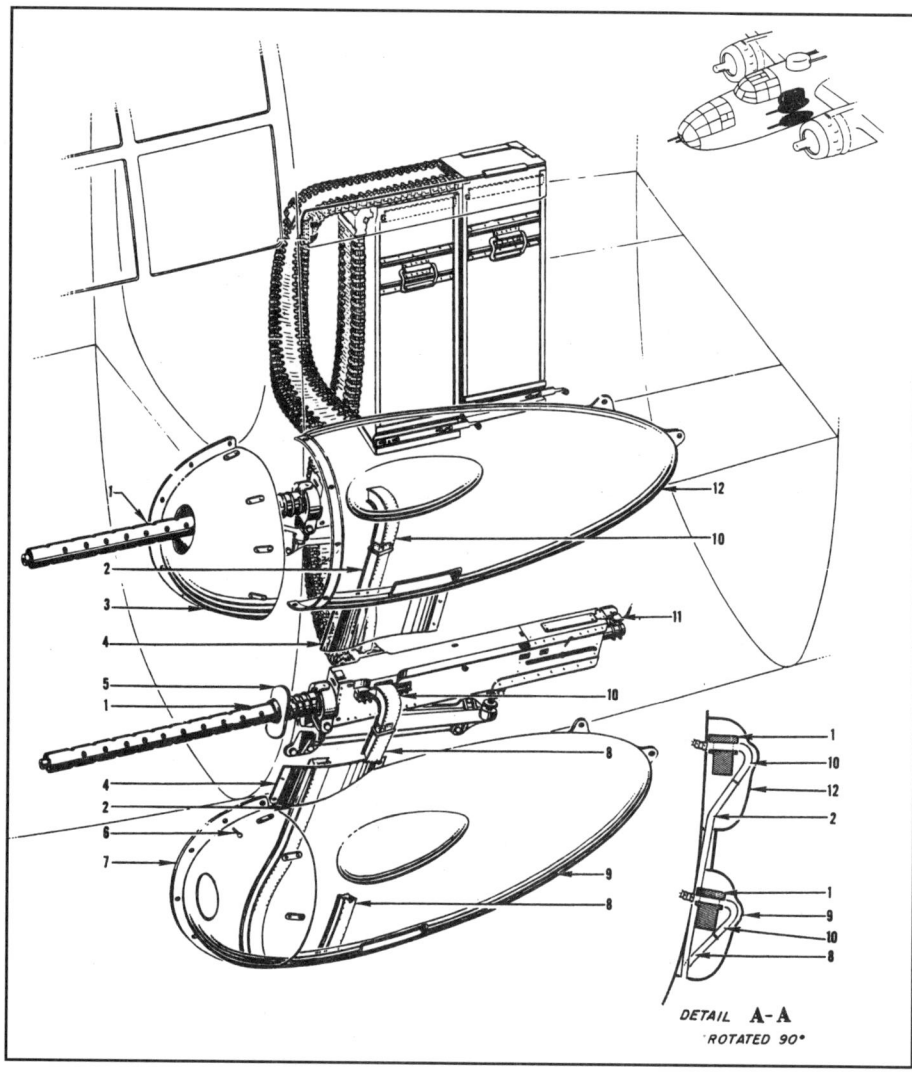

Lefthand package gun drawing also shows detail A-A, with link ejection chute from top gun exiting bottom gun blister. (Bill Miranda collection)

out by airmen who had a big picture view, rather than in small piecemeal lots to several ground officers.[4]

The availability of close air support aircraft like the A-36 and bomb-carrying P-40s, P-47s, and P-51s during World War Two probably reduced the close air support mission for twins like the B-25, placing the Mitchell even more squarely in the interdiction role, behind enemy lines, instead of right over the battlefield. Nonetheless, Mitchells were called upon to support specific battlefield situations on occasion.

Perhaps due to the signal importance placed on strategic bombardment by the pre-war Air Corps and the wartime USAAF, medium bombers like the B-25 Mitchell, while receiving a measure of justly deserved fame, did not achieve the same icon status as did heavies like the B-17. One AAF leader who understood the potency of mediums like the B-25 was Gen. George C. Kenney, commander of the Fifth Air Force in the Pacific during many World War Two combat actions.

Kenney's war was fought with ingenuity and adaptability, and the B-25

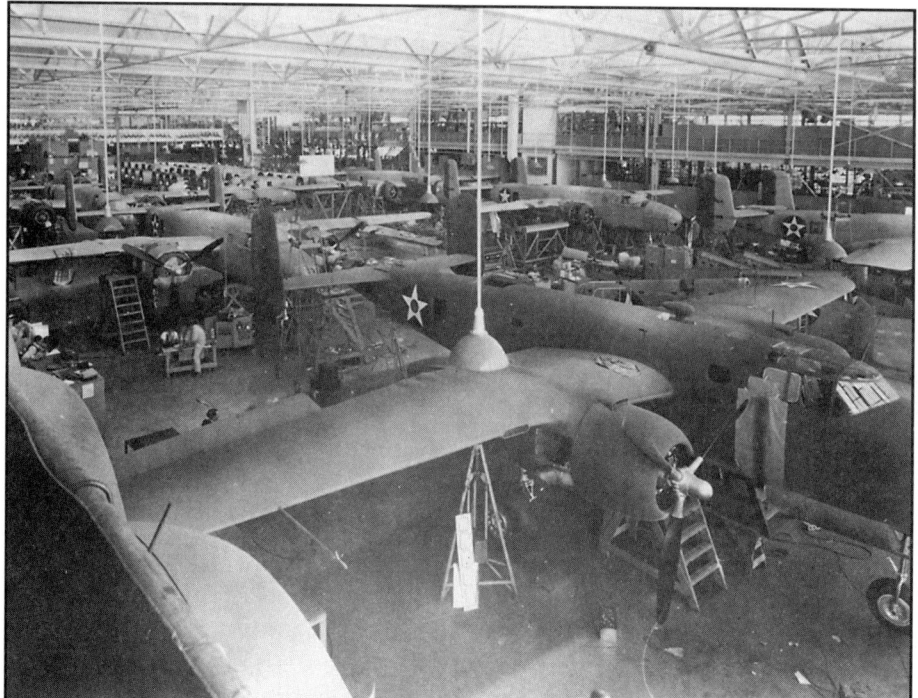

Pre-war B-25 production at Inglewood was big for its day, yet looks like a cottage craft when compared with later wartime mass production operations. Some parts were hand fitted. Mitchell nearest camera does not have leading edge landing lights installed, as do the remainder of the aircraft visible in the photo. (SDAM)

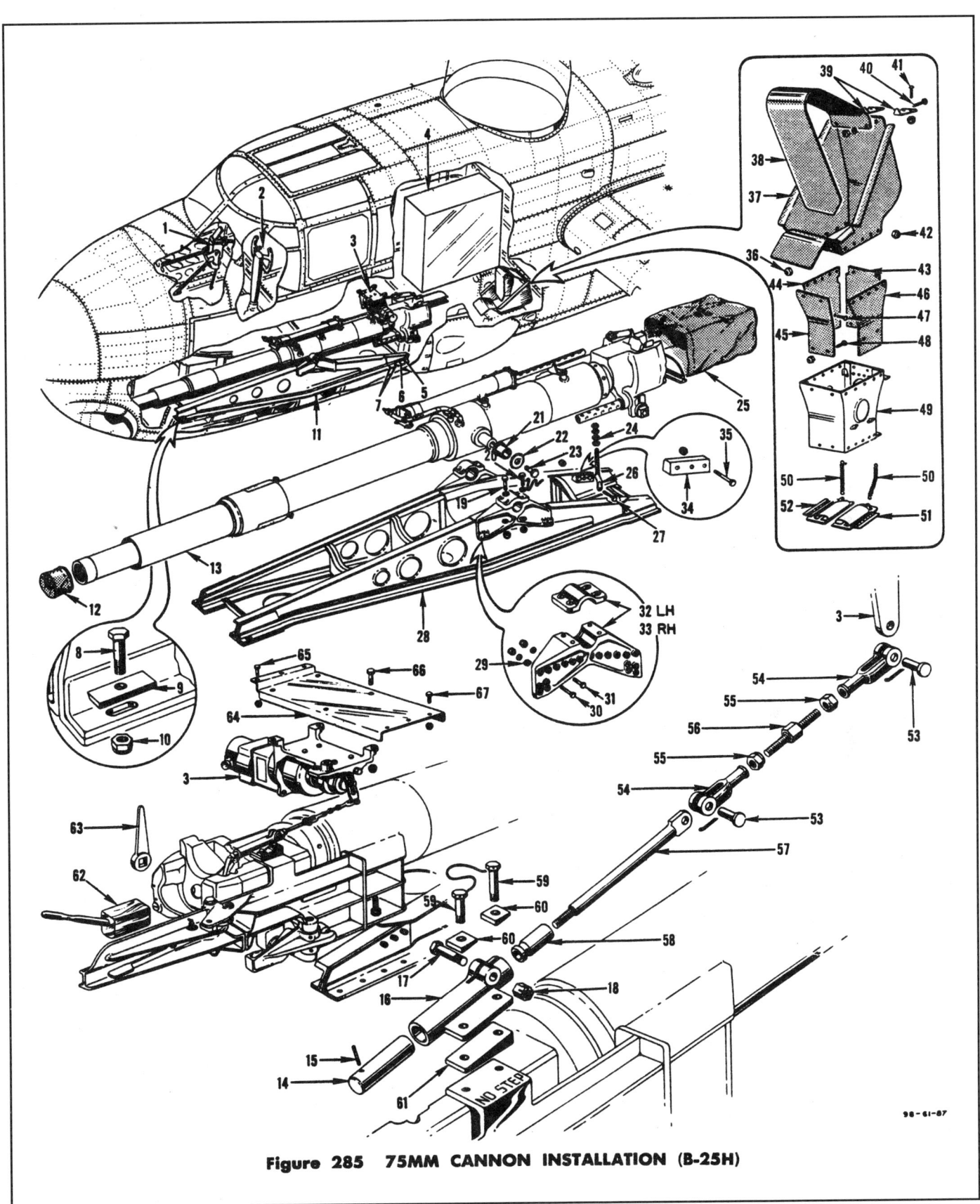

Figure 285 75MM CANNON INSTALLATION (B-25H)

The 75MM cannon installation in the B-25H consumed the traditional crawlspace to the nose. (Bill Miranda collection)

B-25J 44-29259 came equipped with a flexible machine gun in the nose and two fixed nose guns in the left side of the bombardier's compartment; some J-models had only one fixed gun in the nose to complement the flexible 'fifty. Cloth boots sealed weather from the waist and tail gun ports. (NAA/SDAM)

complemented these traits. Low-level attacks on Japanese airfields kept Kenney's bombers hidden from Japanese gunners until the last minute; parachute-retarded bombs allowed the low fliers to escape their own blasts. The Mitchell excelled in this environment. But early Pacific B-25s could be improved with more withering forward firepower to direct against Japanese ground targets and many kinds of shipping.

Enter Paul I. "Pappy" Gunn. Following the successful mounting of four .50-caliber machine guns in the noses of Fifth Air Force A-20 Havocs, Gunn repeated and enlarged on his accomplishment by turning a B-25C into a "commerce destroyer" at the behest of General Kenney in November 1942. Again, four .50-calibers replaced the bombardier in the Plexiglas nose of the Mitchell, but the B-25 conversion outdid the Havoc by adding a pair of .50-caliber machine guns on each side of the fuselage beneath the cockpit, and three more of the weapons beneath the fuselage, all aimed forward to hose bullets at Japanese ships.[5]

The belly guns on the Fifth Air Force commerce destroyer testbed had a bad habit of causing one of the nosewheel doors to fly off the Mitchell whenever they were fired; ultimately they were deleted, for this and reasons of weight and rivet fatigue. With revisions to accommodate center of gravity changes, and installation of rubber padding to damp the rivet-popping vibration of the added guns, Pappy Gunn's strafer B-25 was ready for trial by fire.[6]

Kenney envisioned this Mitchell conversion as performing anti-aircraft fire suppression by blasting the decks of Japanese ships with concentrated machine gunfire on the run in to drop bombs that would ultimately dispatch the vessels. In December 1942, General Kenney recalled, he flew to Brisbane to see how Pappy Gunn's commerce destroyer was progress-

B-25A photographed at pre-war exhibit repeated its tail code — 65 10AB — on the undersurfaces of the wings. Large single exhaust stack common to early Mitchells is visible on side of nacelle. (SDAM)

Used for depicting armament in B-25 and B-25A models, an early drawing was based on the unbroken wing line of the first nine aircraft built. Flexible .30-caliber guns could be moved from socket to socket in the nose — not a very practical combat option. (Carl Scholl/Aero Trader)

ing. Obviously nose heavy, the aircraft was ultimately improved by moving the side package guns back about three feet, relocating their ammunition sources in the bomb bay, and putting lead in the tail.[7] The B-25 commerce destroyer was a resounding success, leading ultimately to factory-built versions of the package guns appearing on glass-nosed B-25Js as well as solid-nosed gunships.

The influence of Gen. George Kenney and Paul "Pappy" Gunn on the evolution and use of the

Classic frontal view of straight-wing B-25 of the 17th Bomb Group, at Felts Field, Spokane, Washington, in 1941 shows crank-winged Mitchells behind it. (Photo by Boardman C. Reed via Peter M. Bowers)

B-25 (no suffix letter) of the 95th Bomb Squadron, 17th Bomb Group, came to grief on 27 September 1941. Large streamlined engine nacelles housed mainwheels. (SDAM)

B-25 profoundly improved the Mitchell's capability as an interdiction weapon. Kenney also fostered the use of parafrag bombs — originally using up old supplies of 23-pound bombs he had rigged with parachutes back in 1928 — to sow destruction among parked Japanese aircraft. If the Mitchell was a worthy bomber around the world, the men of Kenney's Fifth Air Force made it even more so by their ingenuity and courage in the execution of mast-high strikes against Japanese shipping.

The B-25 Mitchell was a useful arrow in the quiver of the World

B-25J rendering shows basic layout and equipment. (NAA/Gene Boswell)

War Two U.S. Army Air Forces, adding diversity to the capabilities of what was to become the strongest aerial force in the world.

EXPERT OPINION

More than a half century after the last B-25 leaped from the Kansas City airfield where it was manufactured, Mitchells remain favorites in the high-stakes warbird market. At Aero Trader in Chino, California, Carl Scholl and Tony Ritzman head a team of warbird rebuilders whose specialty is known worldwide to be B-25 Mitchells. Scholl, who estimated in 1997 that he had worked on 15 to 20 Mitchell projects, said: "Overall it's a very well-designed airplane from an engineering and maintenance standpoint... North American had some very good engineers working for them."[8]

Early Mitchells, through the B-model, had a few quirks, including a complicated system of bellcranks and push rods to transmit engine control inputs, later changed to more standard pulleys and cables. But with the definitive combat-proven C-model, "they really cleaned the airplane up," he added. Scholl said the B-25 is representative of other North American Aviation warplanes of the era — easy to maintain and long-lasting, with "no evil flight characteristics." In Carl Scholl's studied opinion, it is no fluke that a hefty portion of surviving warbirds in the late 1990s are North American Aviation products, be they B-25s, P-51s, AT-6s, or T-28s.[9]

---

[1] Eduard Mark, *Aerial Interdiction in Three Wars*, Center for Air Force History, Washington, DC, 1994. [2] Ray Wagner, *American Combat Planes*, Doubleday, Garden City, NY, 1968. [3] *Ibid.* [4] Eduard Mark, *Aerial Interdiction in Three Wars*, Center for Air Force History, Washington, DC, 1994. [5] Steve Birdsall, *Flying Buccaneers — The Illustrated Story of Kenney's Fifth Air Force*, Doubleday, Garden City, NY, 1977. [6] *Ibid.* [7] George C. Kenney, *General Kenney Reports*, Duell, Sloan, and Pearce, New York, 1949; reprinted by Office of Air Force History, Washington, DC, 1987. [8] Interview, author with Carl Scholl, July 1997. [9] *Ibid.*

DESIGN AND DEVELOPMENT

EACH MODEL MEETS A NEED

Production of B-25 bombers reached 9,816 examples built between 1940 and 1945[1], with more than 8,000 of these seeing service with the U.S. Army Air Forces (USAAF). In 1938, North American Aviation (NAA) engineers began laying out the design of a twin-engine medium bomber in the hope of meeting an Air Corps requirement set forth that year. A company-funded prototype, given NAA model number NA-40-1, used angular twin tails and tricycle landing gear, and a narrow, deep fuselage with a long greenhouse cockpit canopy somewhat like a cross between an exaggerated O-47 observation aircraft's and a Douglas A-20's to complete the look. A pair of 1100-horsepower R-1830 engines did not deliver the kind of performance that would make this design a clear winner when it first flew in January 1939, so a switch to Wright R-2600s of (initially) 1350 horsepower was made, along with a designation change sometimes reported as NA-40B and other times listed as NA-40-2.

Delivered to Wright Field quickly in March of 1939, the uprated NA-40B underwent only two weeks of testing before crashing. The same rapid pace of advancement and development that saw the prototypes of the P-38 and B-17 crash without resulting in termination of those projects found the twin-engine NAA bomber still alive in the imagination of the Air Corps. But changes were wanted, and NAA engineers including J. Lee Atwood and R.H. Rice took some features of the NA-40 and reshaped and widened the fuselage, metamorphosing the design into NAA model NA-62, the first B-25.

The engines by now were R-2600-9 variants producing 1,700 horsepower each, and the gross weight had crept up to more than 27,000 pounds from the original NA-40's 19,500 pounds. The wing of the NA-62 was mounted lower than that of the NA-40, and, by virtue of the wider fuselage, the NA-62's wingspan grew by a foot and a half to 67 feet, six inches.[2]

When the Army took delivery of the first nine B-25s without any suffix letter (known by the North American Aviation factory model number 62), these aircraft had constant dihedral from the root to the tip of

The NA-62 underwent vertical tail evolution. When photographed on the textured surface of Rogers Dry Lake (Muroc Army Air Base) before World War Two, the NA-62 had squared vertical tails. (Peter M. Bowers collection)

With rounded tails smaller than the final variant, the NA-62, with constant dihedral, posed for the NAA camera. Tail bumper later would be enclosed in streamlined fairing on production Mitchells. (Bowers collection)

the wings. An undesirable wallowing degradation in directional stability on these nine B-25s prompted NAA engineers to test a B-25 model in the University of Washington's Kirsten Wind Tunnel. As related in 1988 by a former wind tunnel engineering aide, at the end of a disappointing day of test runs, the NAA engineer told the wind tunnel workers to cut the wings off outboard of the engines and remount them on the elegant wooden scale model with reduced dihedral.[3] The idea worked; subsequent B-25s were characterized by a gull-wing appearance.

The gull appearance was exaggerated by the noticeable dihedral remaining inboard of the engines, plus the natural tapering in thickness which made the upper surfaces of the wings appear to droop even more. The positive dihedral at the intersection of the chord plane

The first B-25 (40-2165), Model NA-62, showing pre-production tail configuration, bulging tail gun emplacement, and constant wing dihedral. (N.L. Avery/SDAM)

NORTH AMERICAN B-25 MITCHELL

B-25As seen at March Field, California, in June 1941 showed off the tail gun emplacement which was deleted when first power turrets were added to the B-model. (Peter M. Bowers)

and the leading edge of the center section was a little more than four degrees; the negative dihedral at the intersection of the chord plane and the leading edge of the outer wing panel was only slightly to the minus, measured as zero degrees, 21 minutes and 39 seconds negative.[4]

Fifteen more B-25s were delivered with the cranked wings before production shifted to 40 B-25As with pilot armor and self-sealing gasoline tanks. NAA's design philosophy for the Mitchell compartmentalized the aircraft into 48 major assemblies. This afforded great flexibility as the B-25 adapted throughout World War Two, since changes could be made to specific assemblies without nec-

The B-25B introduced power dorsal and ventral turrets mounting a pair of .50-caliber guns each; this was at first thought sufficient to warrant deletion of the tailguns. B-model retained single exhaust stack. (N.L. Avery / SDAM)

18

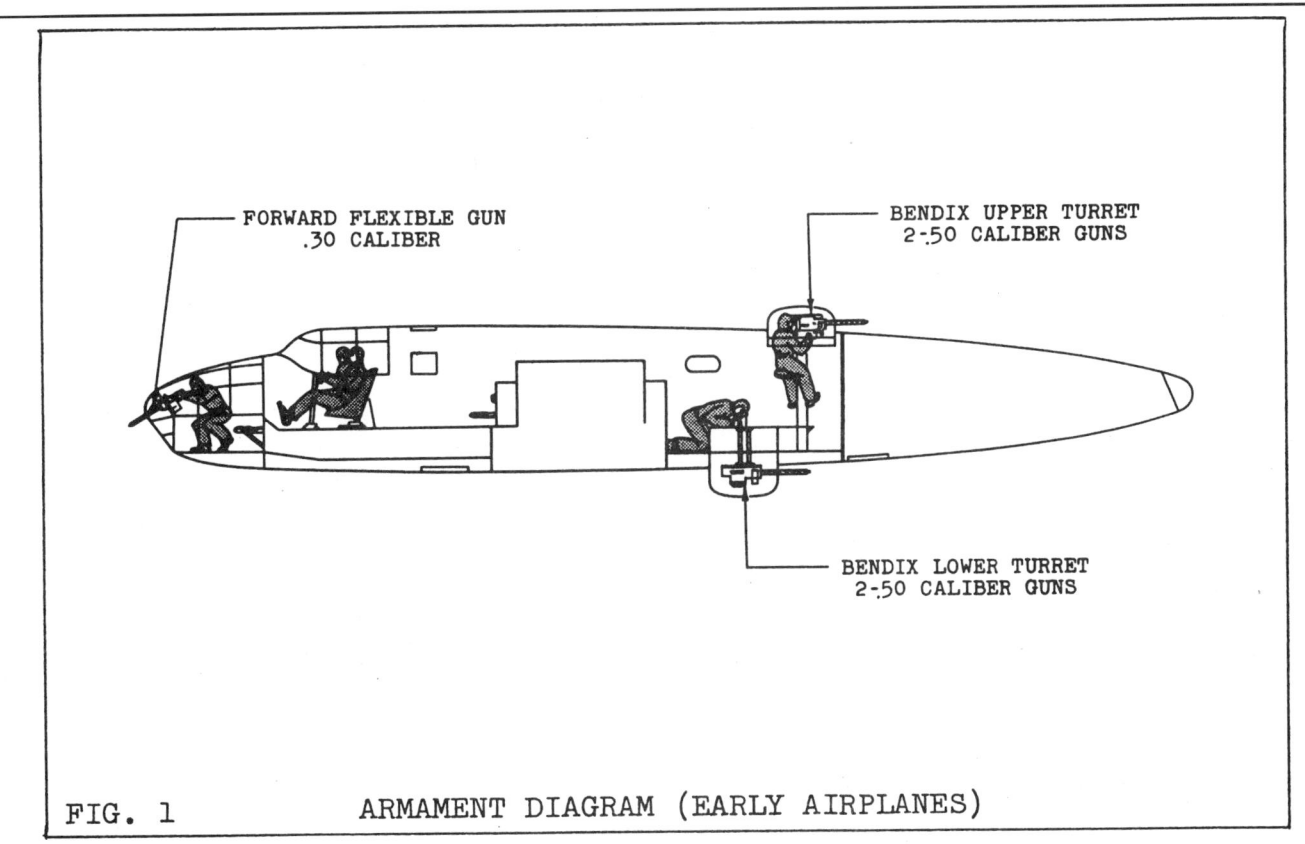

FIG. 1   ARMAMENT DIAGRAM (EARLY AIRPLANES)

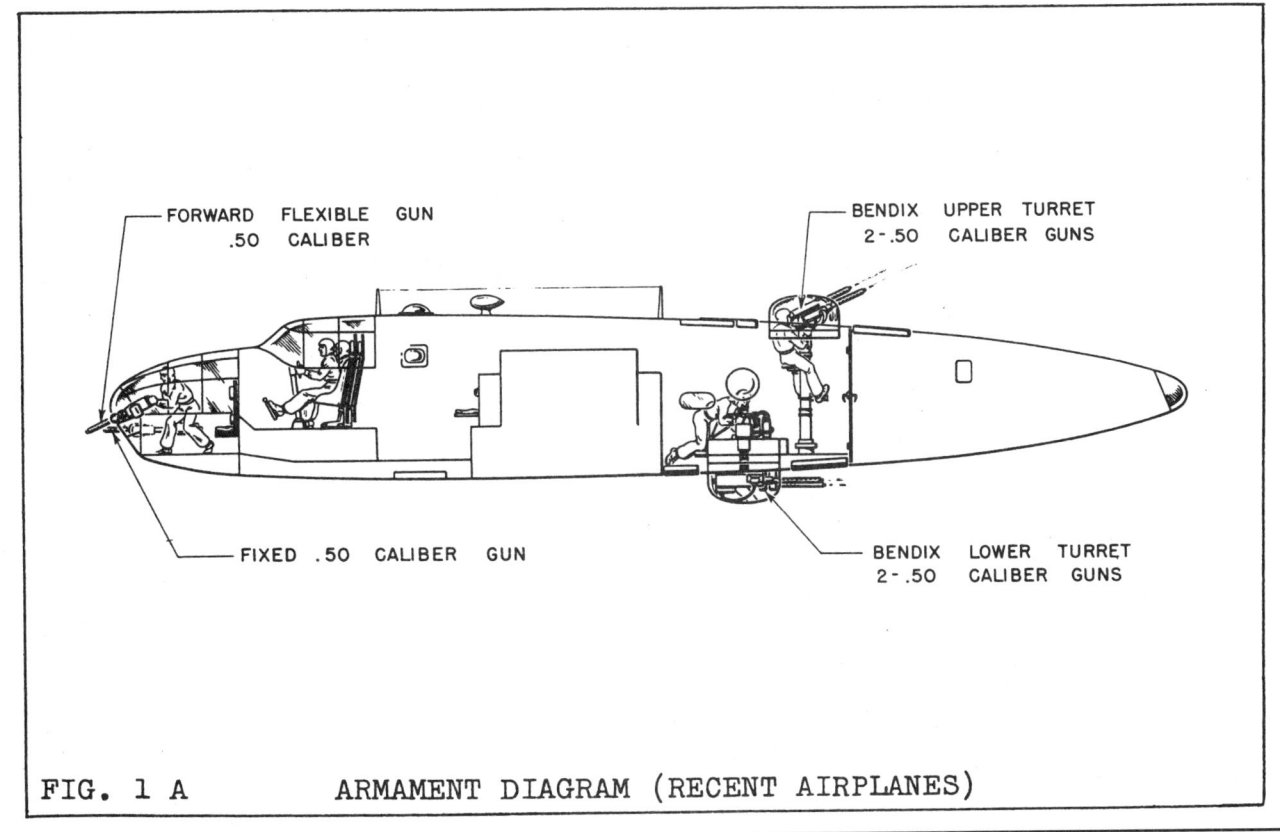

FIG. 1 A   ARMAMENT DIAGRAM (RECENT AIRPLANES)

The advent of power turrets with the B-25B included a cumbersome retractable belly turret at which the gunner kneeled. (Carl Scholl/Aero Trader)

Nose down, an early Mitchell (possibly a B-model) suffered sheared rivets and torn skin in a mishap that looked to be reparable. (SDAM/Perry)

essarily requiring rework of the rest of the airframe.[5]

The experienced 17th Bomb Group at McChord Field, near Tacoma, Washington, was the first unit to go operational with B-25s in 1941. As B-25 production continued, the 120 B-models (only 119 were delivered; one crashed) introduced electrically-driven Bendix upper and lower turrets each mounting a pair of .50-caliber machine guns. The retractable lower turret bore a strong family resemblance to Bendix turrets that later would adorn B-17s as frontal chin turrets. With the addition of these power turrets, the earlier tail gun installation was deleted on the B-25B. The Royal Air Force obtained 23 B-model Mitchells under Lend-Lease; the Soviet Union also took delivery of a few, sometimes astounding the Americans who turned the B-25s over to the Russians as they watched the Soviets stunt the bombers overhead.

First to see combat, the B-model Mitchell was the variant used by Col. Jimmy Doolittle to strike targets including Tokyo on 18 April 1942 by launching boldly from the aircraft carrier Hornet. To reach their targets and hopefully arrive at Chinese landing fields, the Doolittle B-models were modified at the Northwest Airlines center in Minnesota to tank 1,141 gallons of fuel instead of the normal 694 U.S. gallons.

Before the return of real tail guns to the B-25 line, the Doolittle B-25Bs used large wooden dowels to simulate tail guns.[6]

The improved B-25C of late 1941 was also built at North American's Kansas factory as the similar B-25D. Known by the company as model NA-82, the B-25C featured an autopilot, external racks, and R-2600-13 engines. The underwing racks could mount as many as eight 250-lb. bombs. During

B-25C introduced streamlined fairing for tail bumper; initially, C-models had shorter single exhaust stacks than did earlier models. (NAA/SDAM)

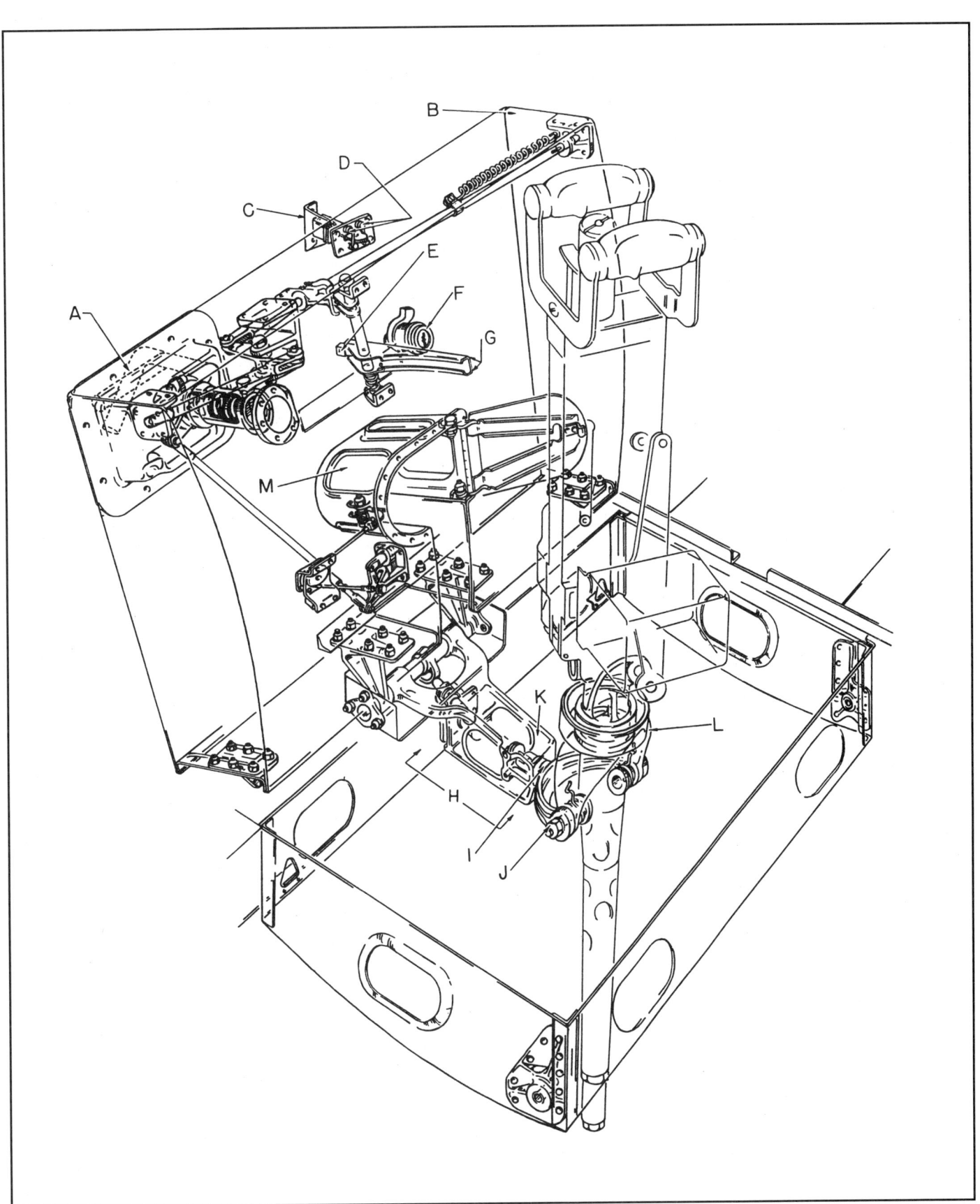

Rear entry hatch on B-25s and B-25As could mount a .30-caliber machine gun, as depicted in an early Mitchell training manual. (Aero Trader)

B-25C variants at Inglewood include USAAF examples with star insignia, as well as Dutch triangle emblem and British roundel. Ventral turret is extended on aircraft nearest to camera. (NAA via Peter M. Bowers)

production of B-25Cs and Ds, increases in wing and fuselage fuel tankage brought the capacity up to 1,100 gallons, nearly as much as was carried by the specialized Doolittle B-models. C- and D-model Mitchells swelled the ranks, with 1,619 B-25Cs leaving Inglewood and 2,290 B-25Ds coming from Kansas City, Kansas.

LATER MITCHELLS

The first time the X-for-experimental designator was applied to a Mitchell was on the XB-25E, a modified C-model that demonstrated hot-air de-icing of the wing leading edge. New electric de-icing equipment was tested on the XB-25F, another former C-model, while another B-25C became the XB-25G with the installation of a huge Army 75-millimeter field gun in the nose, using the crawlspace formerly needed by the bombardier to move to and from the glazed nose in earlier B-25 models. Two .50-caliber machine guns shared the blunt metallized nose on 405 production B-25Gs; these machine guns could be used to help aim the M-4 cannon. A thousand B-25Hs, using the T-13E1

B-25D photographed at Wright Field was similar in many respects to C-model Mitchell. During the production of C and D-model Mitchells, individual exhaust stubs were introduced, replacing the large stacks. (Air Force / SDAM)

Side view of XB-25G shows streamlined fairing cap over gaping muzzle of 75MM cannon in lower left side of nose. The cap had petals that opened to expose the cannon's muzzle; it was not adopted for production versions. (USAAF/Bowers)

75-mm cannon, followed in production, using a total of four blister, or package, guns mounted externally on the fuselage and aimed forward for attacking ground or shipping targets. Four nose-mounted machine guns added to the potential for mayhem in the path of a B-25H. The cannon-toting H-model also re-introduced tail guns as a factory item, and relocated the top turret from a waist location to a spot just aft of the cockpit. Gone for good was the ventral turret, and new to the B-25H and J-models were enlarged waist windows with a single .50-caliber gun at each side. Typically, only one waist gunner was carried to operate both guns as needed.

In the cannon-equipped H-model, the cannoneer loaded the cannon and charged the nose machine guns, all of which were fired by the pilot. The tail gun mount of the B-25H and J-models used a Bell M-7 mount for a pair of .50-caliber M-2

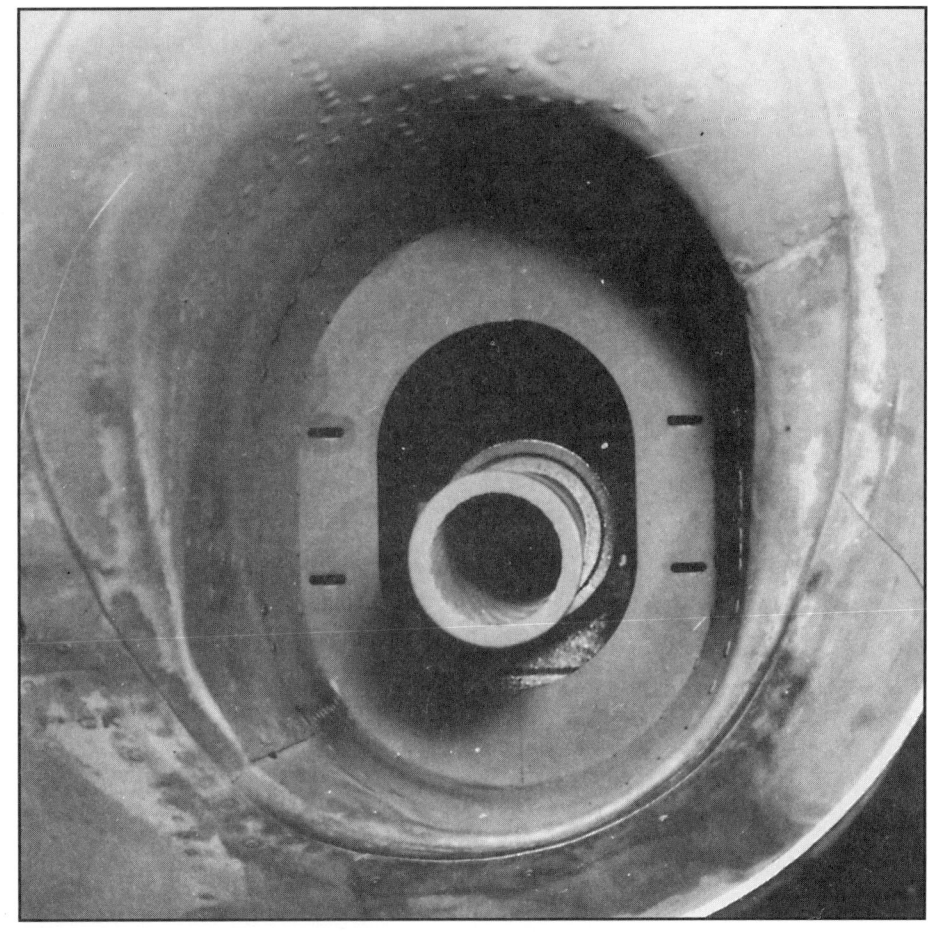

Rifled barrel of 75MM cannon was housed in offset opening, as depicted in this B-25H. (SDAM)

The Air Technical Service Command looked at the possibility of using rocket launchers in place of the 75mm gun on a B-25H. (SDAM)

machine guns. In describing the B-25H and J-models, NAA engineer C.J. Hansen said countersunk rivets were used on the forward third of the fuselage and flying surfaces as a drag reduction measure, with brazier head rivets employed on the aft two-thirds of this structure. The B-25H was credited with a top speed of 293 miles an hour at 13,000 feet; the J-model could attain 292 miles an hour at 14,500 feet. Service ceiling in the H-model was 23,800 feet; for the B-25J, service ceiling was 25,500 feet. Bomb load typically was about one ton.[7]

Cannon-armed Mitchells had their proponents, but the big weapons were not universally favored, and were generally removed from combat later in 1944. Last production model was the glass-nosed B-25J, retaining the package guns as an option, forward location for the dorsal turret, and the raised "doghouse" tail gun emplacement.

To protect the tail gunner from accidental "cook-off" rounds from the aft-stowed guns of the top turret, two angled plates of armor, faired in rounded aluminum bumps, were placed on top of the fuselage just aft of the turret guns. Sometimes, combat users of late B-25s left the aluminum fairings off the angled armor plates because the aluminum fairings would only be destroyed by a bullet anyway, and might result in undesirable trajectories for cook-off rounds.[8]

B-25G was readily distinguishable from H-model by aft placement of dorsal turret on the G. (NAA)

Views of both sides of B-25H (43-4198) with red-bordered national insignia reveal the slight stagger to the bulged waist windows; note the relative position of the windows on each side to the national insignia.

The B-25J was the most produced variant of the Mitchell, topping out at 4,318 examples delivered by NAA from its Kansas City, Kansas, plant. Many of the J-models replaced Martin B-26 Marauders in the Pacific. As low-level missions made the carrying of a bombardier less necessary, some B-25Js were factory built with an eight-gun solid nose using .50-caliber weapons for deadly powerful strafing.[9]

MITCHELL FIREPOWER AND ORDNANCE EVOLUTION

Evolution of the B-25 series was characterized by an ever-increasing amount of firepower — both offensive and defensive — that was added to the Mitchell's weight, typically as dictated by wartime experience.

The original B-25s (serials 40-2165 - 40-2188) — tabbed RB-25s in a 1945 AAF summary (the R designator indicated an aircraft no longer considered suitable for its original mission) — carried only four machine guns, three of which were .30-caliber weapons. The solo .50-caliber weapon was for tail protection; the .30-calibers were apportioned to the nose, upper rear, and lower rear socket positions. Prewar thinking opined that the nose gun could be switched to any of three sockets in the nose for best use; the lower rear gun likewise was to be placed in side windows if desired. These straight B-25s could carry up to 3,000 pounds of bombs internally, although the design bomb load was 2,000 pounds.[10]

The B-25As (40-2189 - 40-2228) were armed the same as the first straight B-25s had been. First major weaponry changes came about with the B-25B, which sported a Bendix A4 upper turret and an A5 lower turret made by the same company. Each turret used a pair of

Gun-nose B-25J variant could present a total of 14 forward-firing .50-caliber machine guns when top turret was rotated forward, giving a withering hail of fire for attacking targets on land or sea. (NAA)

.50-caliber machine guns; the lone flexible .30-caliber weapon remained in the glazed nose. Bomb loads for A- and B-model Mitchells remained as for earlier variants. The B-25C-NA (41-12434 through 41-13038) carried the same gun complement, but raised the total number of 250-pound bombs that could be carried from six to eight. B-25C-1-NA versions (41-13039 - 41-13296) had the same gun array, but offered revised bomb loads, including the ability to carry six 325-pound depth bombs begin-

B-25H and J-models had a tail gun emplacement with a removable top hatch. A baggy canvas boot enclosed the guns and permitted freedom of movement. (National Archives/Bowers)

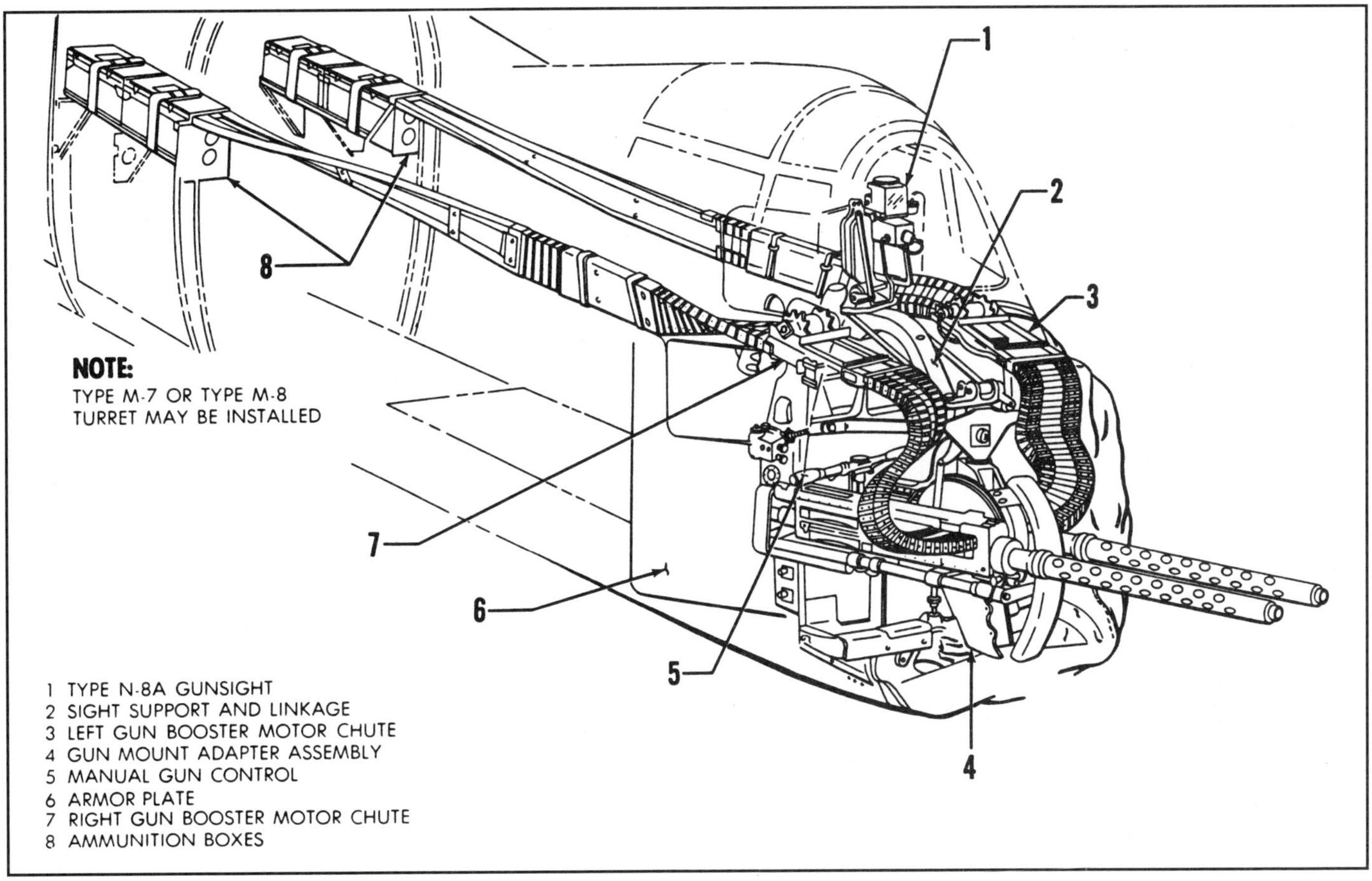

NOTE:
TYPE M-7 OR TYPE M-8
TURRET MAY BE INSTALLED

1. TYPE N-8A GUNSIGHT
2. SIGHT SUPPORT AND LINKAGE
3. LEFT GUN BOOSTER MOTOR CHUTE
4. GUN MOUNT ADAPTER ASSEMBLY
5. MANUAL GUN CONTROL
6. ARMOR PLATE
7. RIGHT GUN BOOSTER MOTOR CHUTE
8. AMMUNITION BOXES

Detailed drawing of B-25J tail gun emplacement, from USAAF B-25J erection and maintenance manual, shows long twisted ammo feed chutes leading from ammo boxes (part number 8). Armor plate (part number 6) protected gunner, although his hands had to reach beyond armor to work the guns. (Keller/Sturges)

ning with aircraft number 41-13196, or, for the entire block, one 2,000-pound torpedo. This production block introduced external underwing bomb racks on the Mitchell series, capable of hauling a total of eight 250-pound bombs.[11]

Although field modifications would alter B-25 armaments in service, as built the B-25C-5-NA (42-53332 - 42-53493) introduced one flexible and one fixed .50-caliber machine gun to the Mitchell's nose, marking the first in the series to do away with small .30-caliber weapons altogether, and pointing the way toward ever-increasing frontal firepower for the B-25. B-25C-10 (42-32233 - 42-32382) and -15 (42-32383 and 42-32389 - 42-32532) blocks were similar in arms to previous C-models. Next production armament change was the introduction of improved A-9

Derelict B-25J carcass showed major production joint in fuselage at front of wing spar. (Frederick A. Johnsen)

Production line view probably depicts B-25H. Visible are mounts for package guns, and blast protection sheets on fuselage. (Rockwell/Gene Boswell)

upper and A-10 lower turrets on the B-25C-20-NA production block (42-64502 - 42-64701). The AAF's armament tally said the B-25C-25-NA (42-64702 - 42-64801) was capable of hauling two 1600-pound bombs internally. Guns remained the same on this block as for the previous production block.[12]

The B-25D-NC, essentially a Kansas City-built equivalent to an early C-model, (41-29648 - 41-29847), was configured with the single .30-caliber flexible nose gun and three sockets for its use. Top turret was the A4 upper on the first 82 aircraft of this block; the remainder used the A-9. Lower turret was the A5 on the first 80 aircraft in this batch; the

Photo of B-25 right main landing gear shows aluminum silver-painted strut, smooth contour (SC) tire. (Rockwell/Gene Boswell)

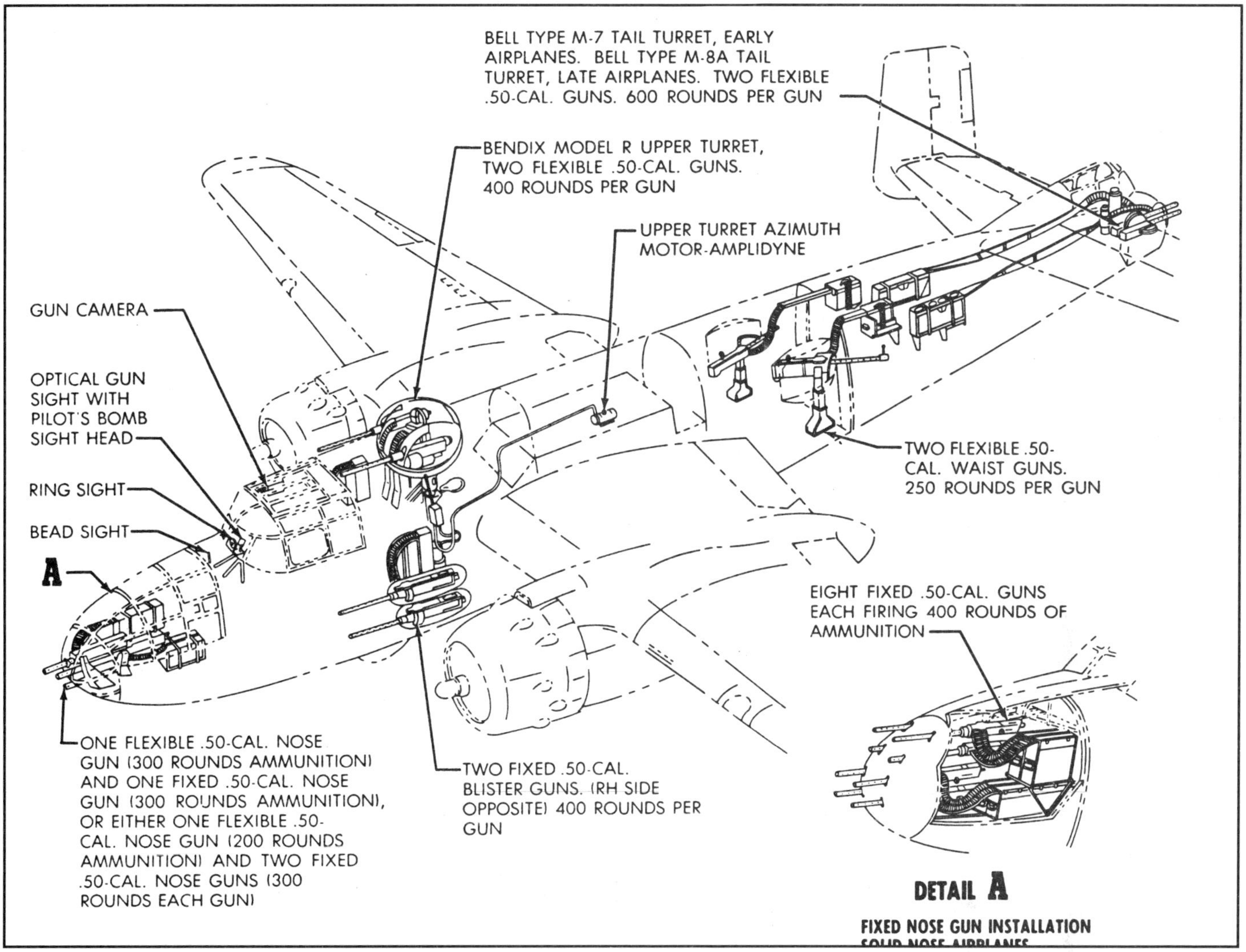

- BELL TYPE M-7 TAIL TURRET, EARLY AIRPLANES. BELL TYPE M-8A TAIL TURRET, LATE AIRPLANES. TWO FLEXIBLE .50-CAL. GUNS. 600 ROUNDS PER GUN
- BENDIX MODEL R UPPER TURRET, TWO FLEXIBLE .50-CAL. GUNS. 400 ROUNDS PER GUN
- UPPER TURRET AZIMUTH MOTOR-AMPLIDYNE
- GUN CAMERA
- OPTICAL GUN SIGHT WITH PILOT'S BOMB SIGHT HEAD
- RING SIGHT
- BEAD SIGHT
- TWO FLEXIBLE .50-CAL. WAIST GUNS. 250 ROUNDS PER GUN
- EIGHT FIXED .50-CAL. GUNS EACH FIRING 400 ROUNDS OF AMMUNITION
- ONE FLEXIBLE .50-CAL. NOSE GUN (300 ROUNDS AMMUNITION) AND ONE FIXED .50-CAL. NOSE GUN (300 ROUNDS AMMUNITION), OR EITHER ONE FLEXIBLE .50-CAL. NOSE GUN (200 ROUNDS AMMUNITION) AND TWO FIXED .50-CAL. NOSE GUNS (300 ROUNDS EACH GUN)
- TWO FIXED .50-CAL. BLISTER GUNS. (RH SIDE OPPOSITE) 400 ROUNDS PER GUN

DETAIL A
FIXED NOSE GUN INSTALLATION SOLID NOSE AIRPLANES

(Above) Guns of a typical B-25J were shown in the erection and maintenance manual. (Keller / Sturges)

Inside the glazed nose of a B-25, the flexible K-4 gun socket mounted a .50-caliber machine gun using a C-19 adapter and an E-11 recoil adapter to damp vibrations. Pulleys and cables helped balance and support the heavy gun. The bomb sight mount was empty when the photo was taken. On the left side wall, a semicircular air vent generic to many types of aircraft was employed. (NAA)

NORTH AMERICAN B-25 MITCHELL

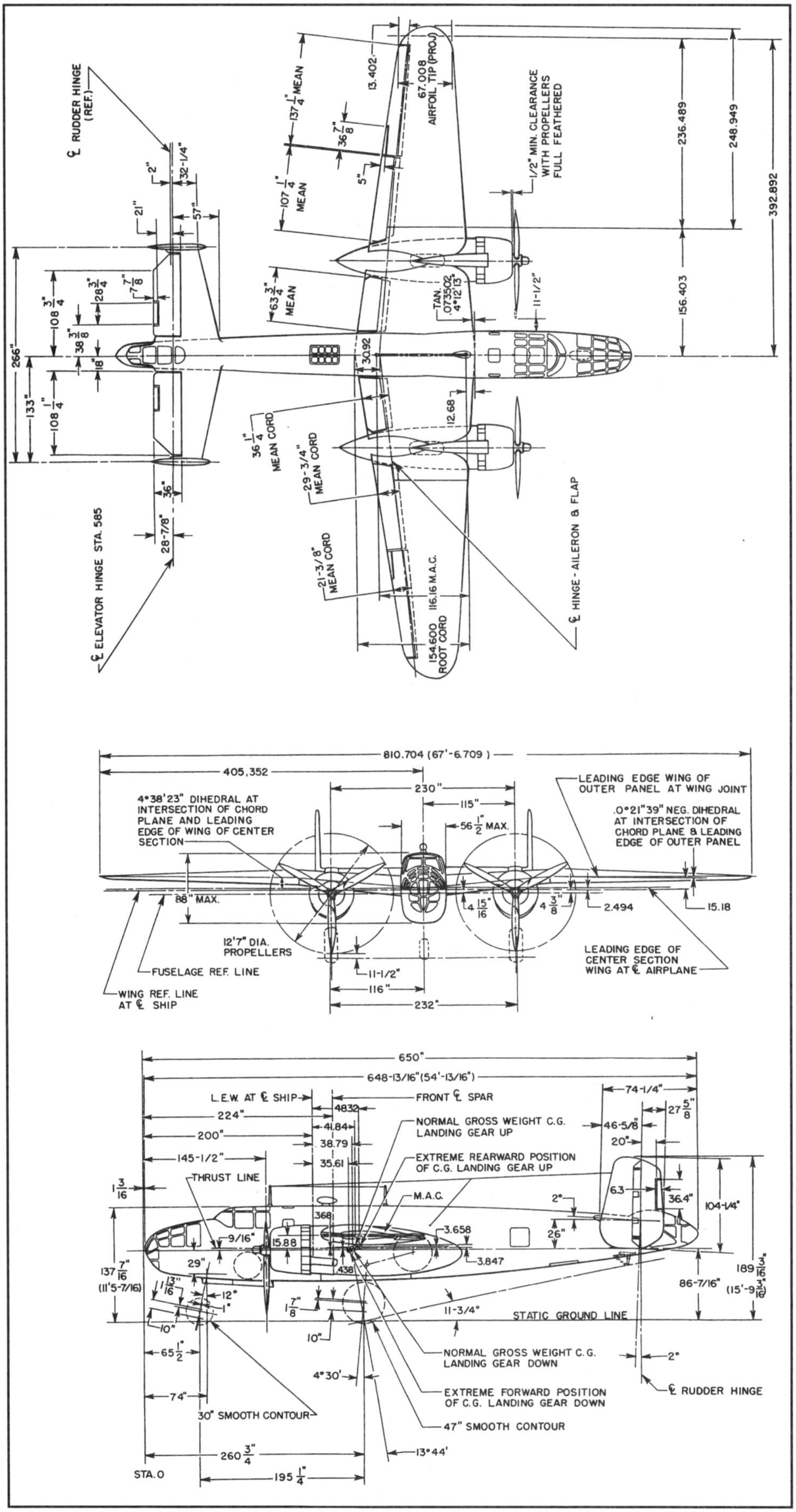

Detailed dimensioned drawings of B-25 and B-25A variants show dorsal hatch and bulbous tail gun emplacement of these earliest Mitchells. (Carl Scholl collection)

remainder used the A-10. On B-25D-1-NC aircraft (41-29848 - 41-29947) Mitchell evolution introduced underwing bomb racks and the ability to carry one torpedo. The B-25D-5-NC marked Kansas City's move to make all Mitchell machine guns .50-caliber, including one fixed and one flexible gun in the glazed nose. B-25D-10-NC versions (41-30173 - 41-30352) were similar in armament to the previous block. Only 100 of the 180 B-25D-15-NC aircraft (41-30353 - 41-30532) were built with the lower turret installed. And 130 of 340 B-25D-20-NC Mitchells (41-30533 - 41-30847, and 42-87113 - 42-87137) carried the lower turret from the factory. Type A-10 lower turrets were installed on all of the B-25D-25-NCs (42-87138 - 42-87452). Armament and bombs remained the same for B-25D-30- and -35-NC Mitchells (42-87453 - 42-8761, 43-3280 - 43-3619, 43-3620 - 43-3869), representing 500 block-30s and 250 block-35s.[13]

The pug-nosed B-25G-1-NA (42-32384 - 42-32388) kept both power turrets of previous models, but drastically altered forward firepower in a stubby aluminum nose, housing two side-by-side fixed .50-caliber machine guns and one hefty M-4 or M-6 75-mm cannon. The cannon was supplied with 21 rounds. Bomb capacity was unchanged. The B-25G-5-NA (42-64802 - 42-65101) was similar to the first batch of G-models, except only 222 of 300

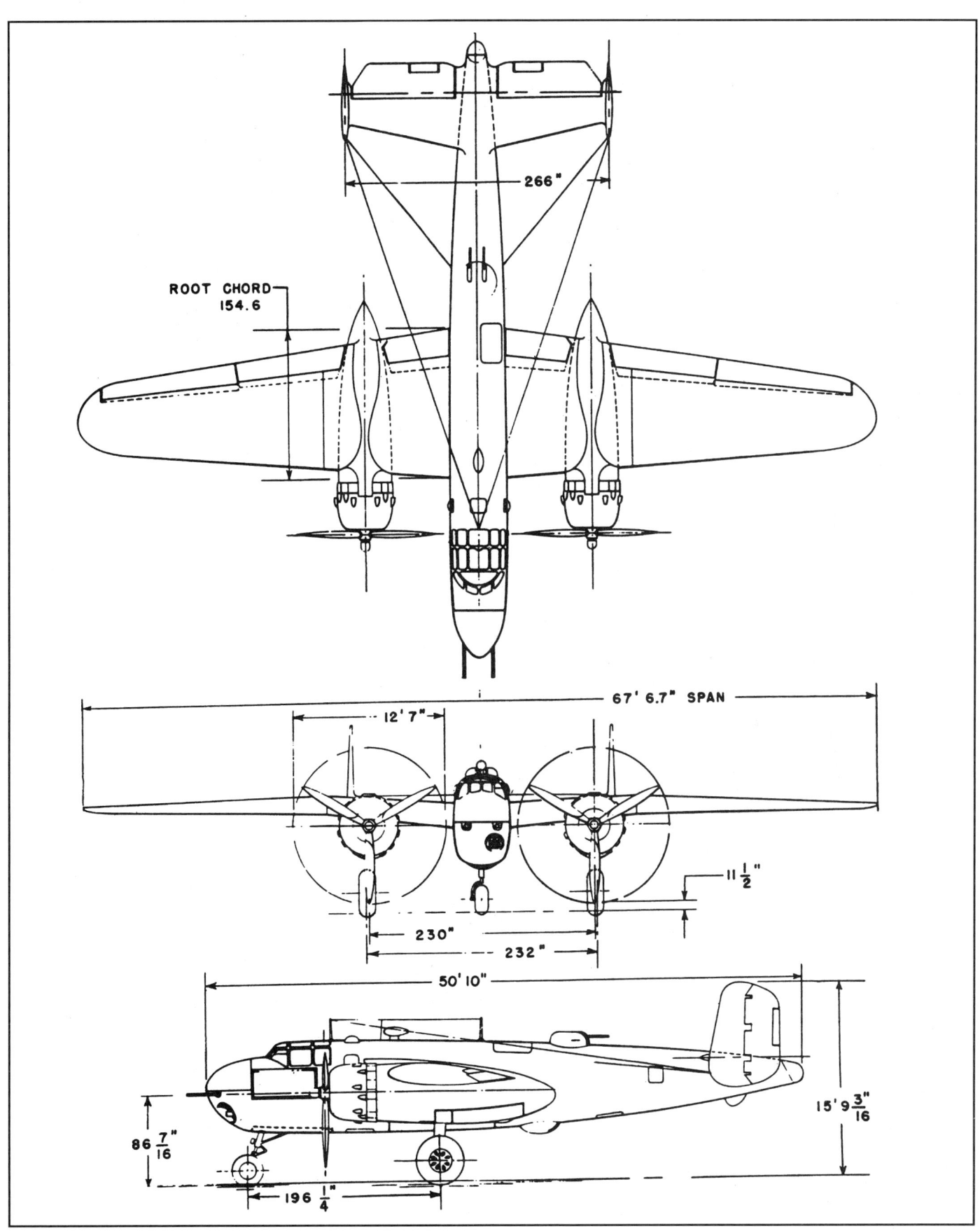

B-25G with 75MM cannon used aft-mounted dorsal turret and only two fixed nose machine guns.

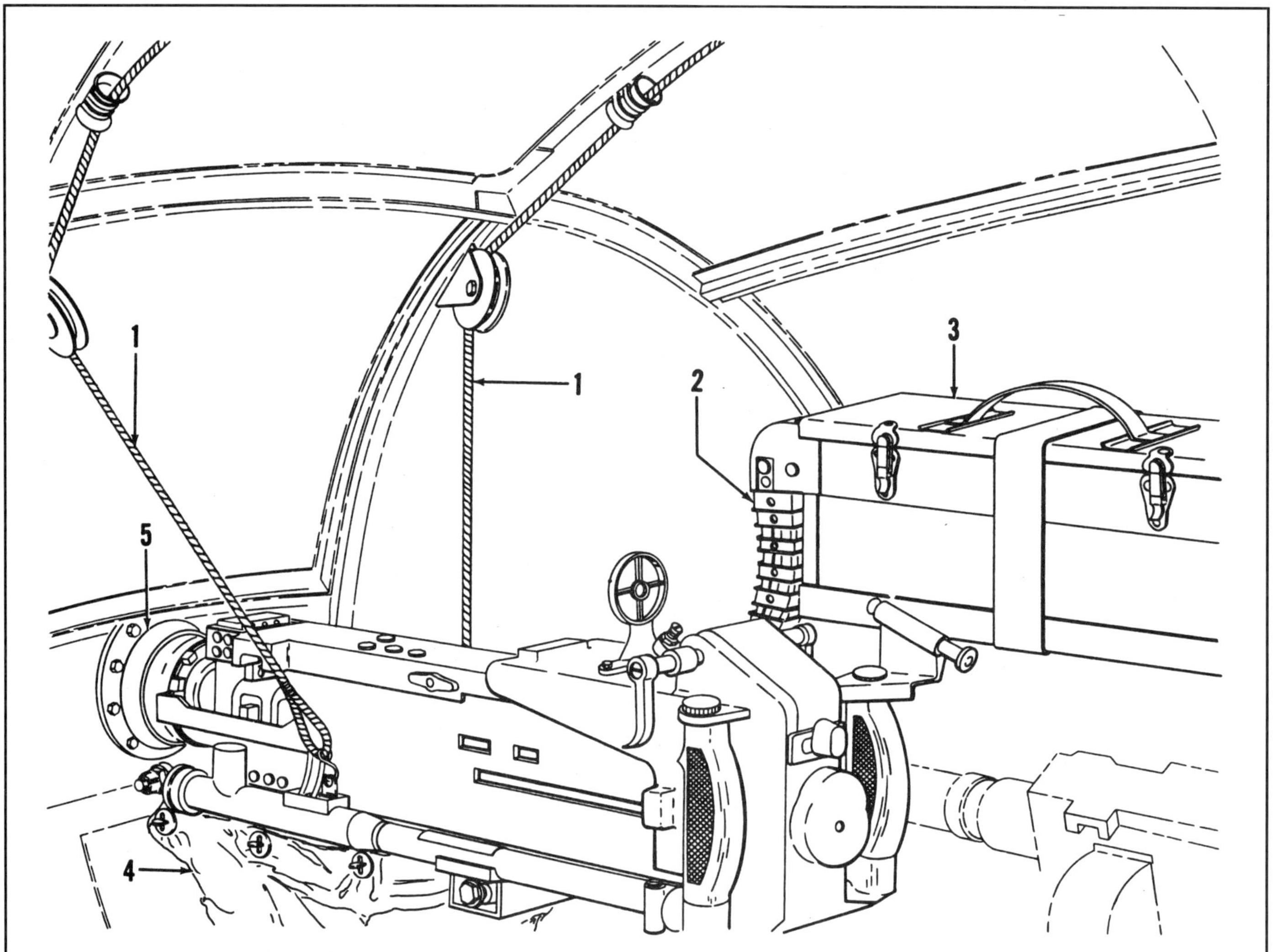

Artwork from a B-25J erection and maintenance manual showed details of the flexible nose gun installation. (Keller/Sturges)

1. BUNGEE ASSEMBLY
2. FLEXIBLE FEED CHUTE
3. AMMUNITION BOXES, CAPACITY 100 ROUNDS EACH
4. CASE AND LINK EJECTION BAG
5. BALL AND SOCKET MOUNT

aircraft in this block had the lower turret installed. The B-25G-10-NA (42-65102 - 42-65201) did away with the lower turret altogether.[14]

Cannon-armed B-25H-1-NAs (43-4105 - 43-4404) represented a definitive armament change for the Mitchell, with two side waist windows each packing a .50-caliber machine gun, an M-7 power-boosted tail gun assembly with a pair of .50-calibers, two package guns on the right side of the nose only, a relocated A-9B top turret, and, typically, a type T13E1 75-mm cannon in the nose. In instances where the T13E1 cannon was unavailable, the M-4 was used in its place; in this M-4 configuration, the outer two nose machine guns were deleted. An AAF armament note said the carriage of a 2,000-pound torpedo precluded closing the bomb bay doors. The subsequent B-25H-5-NA (43-4405 - 43-4704) carried the full four-gun nose machine gun complement and the T13E1 cannon, and added two more forward-firing package guns, on the left side of the fuselage. Beginning with the 131st aircraft of the block-5 H-models, the ability to carry a 2,000-pound bomb was deleted. The B-25H-10-NA (43-4705 - 43-5104) continued the armament of the prior batch.[15]

Considered by some to be the definitive Mitchell, the B-25J returned to the use of a Plexiglas bombardier nose and all-.50-caliber

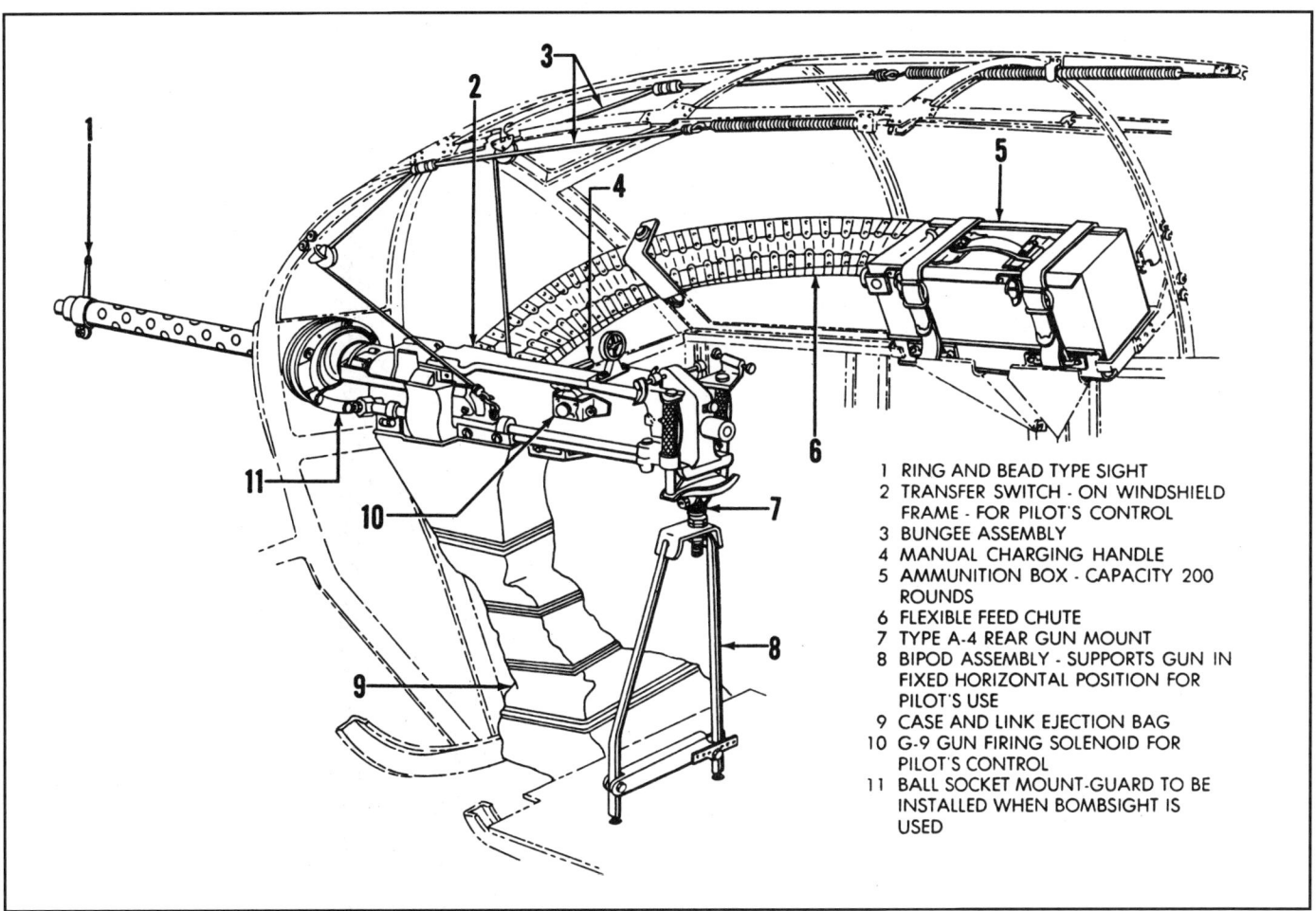

A bipod could be used to fix the flexible nose gun's position for remote forward firing by the B-25 pilot, as depicted in a B-25J erection and maintenance manual. (Keller/Sturges)

guns. On the B-25J-1-NA (43-3870 - 43-4104, 43-27473 - 43-27792) four package guns, one fixed nose gun, and one flexible nose gun could fire forward; waist, upper turret, and tail guns remained as on late H-models. An AAF notation in a B-25J-1-NA armament survey said: "One additional fixed nose gun will be installed at modification centers." The 2,000-pound bomb station was deleted beginning with the 151st B-25J-1-NA. (Two fixed nose guns later became a production feature on some Kansas City J-models). B-25J-5-NC Mitchells (43-27793 - 43-28112) were similar to Inglewood's block-1 J-models. The B-25J-10-NC (43-28113 - 43-28222, 43-35946 - 43-36245) retained similar gun use; added for the first time on J-models was the underwing bomb capability. Starting with the 1,036th B-25J built, the ability to carry six 325-pound depth bombs was reinstated. Similar in armament was the B-25J-15-NC (44-28711 - 44-29110). The B-25J-20-NC (44-29111 - 44-29910) made two fixed nose guns a factory standard, a practice followed on the B-25J-25-NC (44-29911 - 44-30910); B-25J-30-NC (44-30911 - 44-31510, 44-86692 - 44-86891); and finally the B-25J-35-NC (44-86892 - 44-86897, 45-8801 - 45-9242). (Note: B-25J production actually terminated before all of these serial numbers were used; highest number allocated to an airframe was 45-8899, which was among 72 J-models completed but not delivered.) An AAF armament notation reported the last 667 B-25Js built had an M-8A tail gun mount instead of the M-7. As early as B-25J-1 production, an AAF armament note said some of these variants would have a .50-caliber eight-gun solid nose installed at the factory. A thousand such kits were procured. The AAF armament survey also noted: "Five-hundred zero-length rocket launcher kits (were) procured for service installation on B-25 airplanes."[16]

EARLY B-25 ARMAMENT

The first B-25s and B-25As reflected an almost universal naivete about

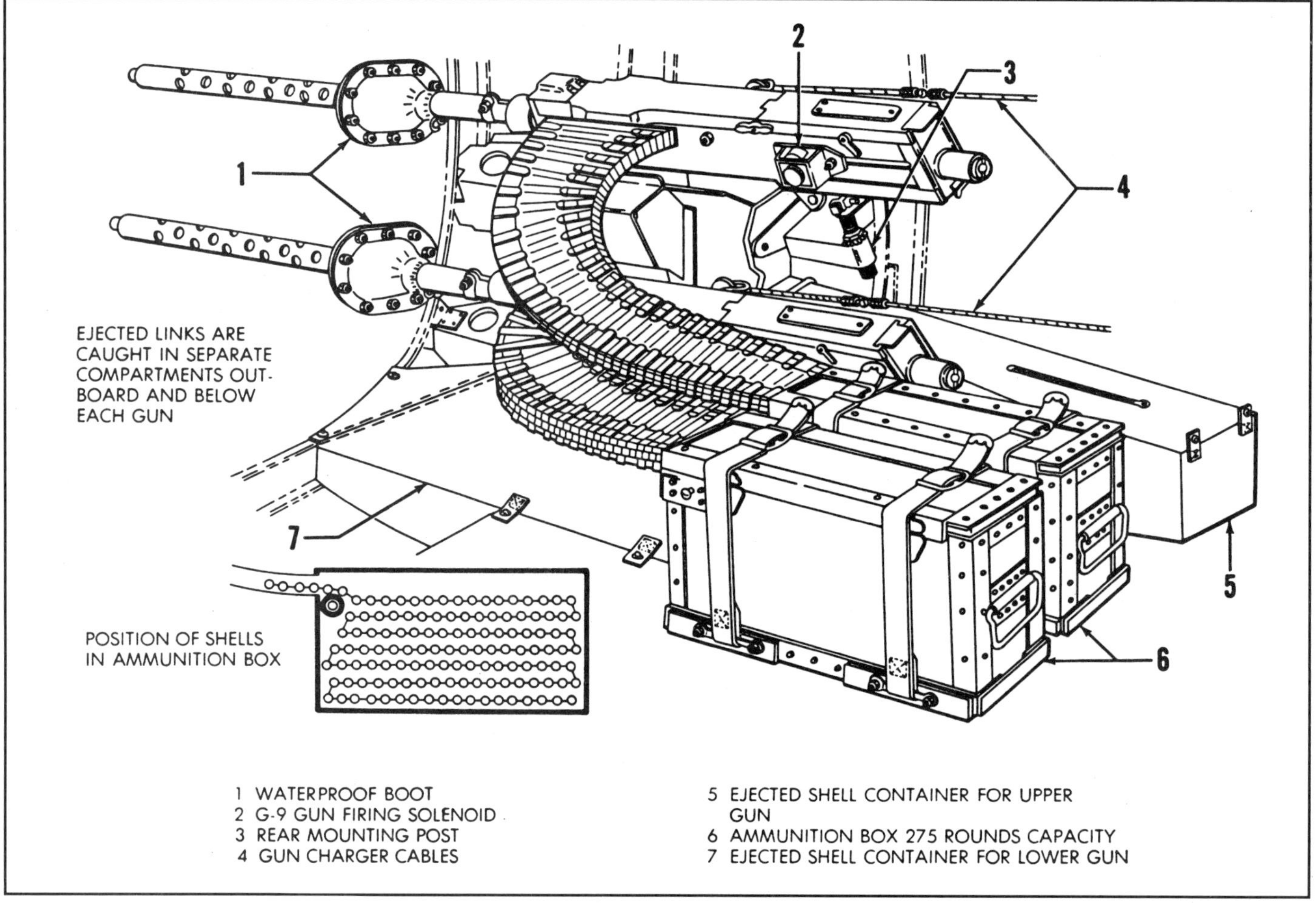

EJECTED LINKS ARE CAUGHT IN SEPARATE COMPARTMENTS OUTBOARD AND BELOW EACH GUN

POSITION OF SHELLS IN AMMUNITION BOX

1 WATERPROOF BOOT
2 G-9 GUN FIRING SOLENOID
3 REAR MOUNTING POST
4 GUN CHARGER CABLES
5 EJECTED SHELL CONTAINER FOR UPPER GUN
6 AMMUNITION BOX 275 ROUNDS CAPACITY
7 EJECTED SHELL CONTAINER FOR LOWER GUN

Some glass-nosed B-25s were fitted with two fixed nose guns, protruding from canvas boots in the nose and fed by 275-round ammo boxes, as drawn for the B-25J erection and maintenance manual. (Keller/Sturges)

bomber defense in the time before mass encounters between fighters and bombers became commonplace during World War Two. Normal complement of guns for these first two models of the Mitchell were one .50-caliber and three .30-caliber machine guns.

The lone .50-caliber protected the rear of the B-25, and was housed in a tail stinger, along with boxes containing 200 rounds of ammunition. This gun could be fitted with a type Q-3 fixed telescope gunsight. To operate the tail gun, the seated gunner first had to ratchet open a pair of clamshell doors. The telescope sight was not entirely satisfactory. An accommodation for it was described by NAA: "Due to the Q-3 sight having a 40-degree cone of sight (or 20 degrees in all directions off centerline), and the gun a 60-degree cone of fire, it was necessary to provide a 10-degree overtravel system in the movement between the gun and the sight. This overtravel is incorporated in the arms attached to the gimbal."[17]

In an era before the introduction of flexible ammunition feed chutes and large-capacity ammunition boxes, the small cans mounted, one at a time, to the tailgun limited the amount of fire. In order to change ammo cans while the clamshell doors were open, the gunner was advised to push the rear of the gun as far to his right as possible "in order to have room to pull the ammunition box between the door and the gun." Three of the cans were mounted on each side of the compartment just forward of the gunner's seat. The B-25 and B-25A tail gunner's seat had a folding back which was raised upright after he was seated. Several pieces of armor plate were fitted in the tail gun emplacement.[18]

The .30-caliber machine guns in B-25 and B-25A models were intended to be moved from socket to socket as needed to ward off attackers. Combat experience showed this to be impractical, and guns later were generally mounted

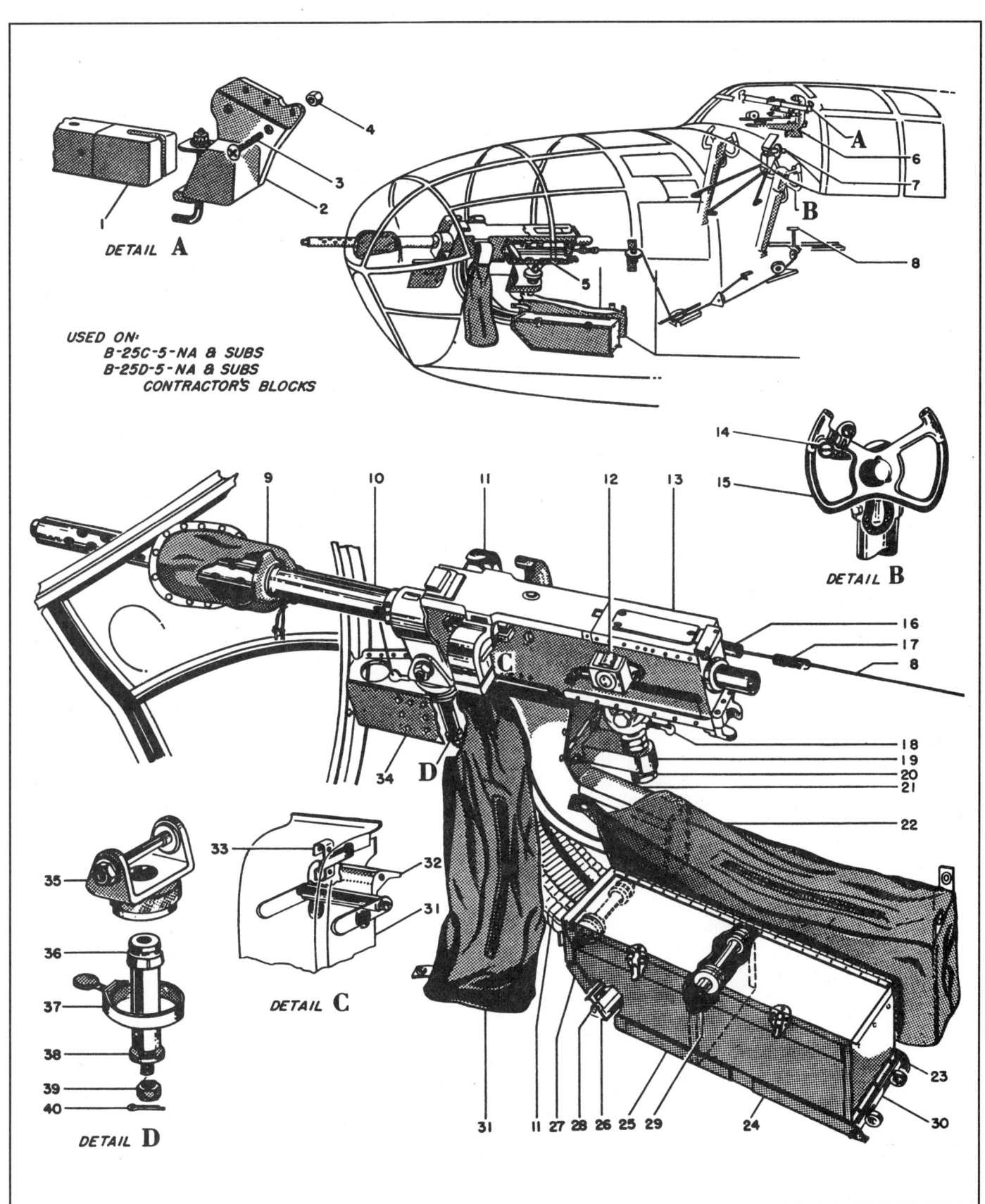

Single fixed nose gun, used on many B-25Cs and Ds, and some J-models, used a cloth bag to catch ejected shell links (part no. 31). Gun was fired by pilot pressing button on left of control column (part no. 14, detail B).

NORTH AMERICAN B-25 MITCHELL

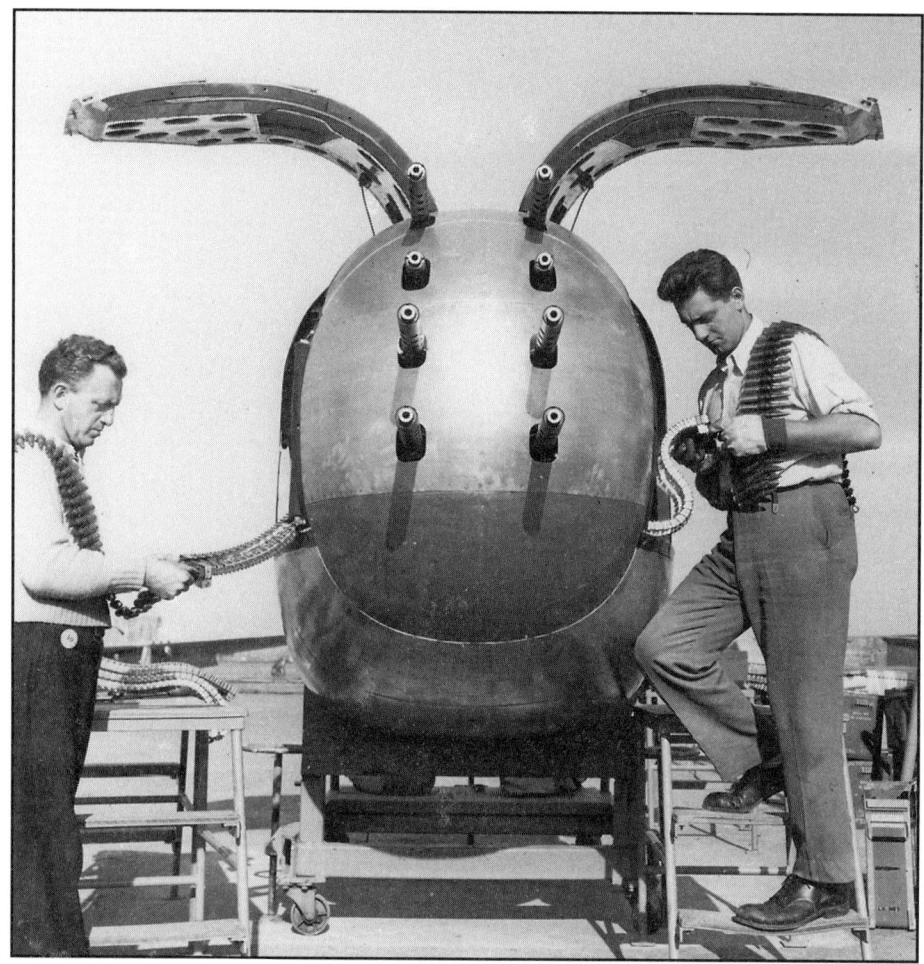

B-25J eight-gun nose on a dolly received .50-caliber ammunition from NAA employees. (NAA)

in all the locations where they were needed. For the early B-25s and B-25As, one small .30-caliber M-2 machine gun was provided for any of three sockets in the Plexiglas-paned nose. Alternately, a type G-4 camera gun could be fitted in the nose gun ball socket. Typically, these early Mitchell .30-caliber weapons used C-12 gun mount adapters and L-4 ammunition box assemblies.[19]

Dorsal protection for B-25s and B-25As was provided by a single .30-caliber gun attached to a floor-mounted post beneath a rectangular window that could be opened in flight. The gunner stood to operate this weapon. He could raise the gun on an extension to obtain a better firing position, and had an extendable wind deflector at his disposal. A safety belt was provided for the top waist gunner. Side waist windows on B-25s and B-25As could take a .30-caliber gun, and the lower waist gun was a ventral opening in the rear entry hatch.[20]

The B-25B introduced power turrets to the Mitchell series, thereby deleting the waist and tail guns. The retractable Bendix ventral turret was in essence a forerunner of the Bendix chin turret popularized on the later B-17G Fly-

A wood plug blocked the central insert in this B-25C's (42-53411) instrument panel photographed at Mather Field, California. Fluorescent lamps were available on control columns of this Mitchell. (USAAF/SDAM)

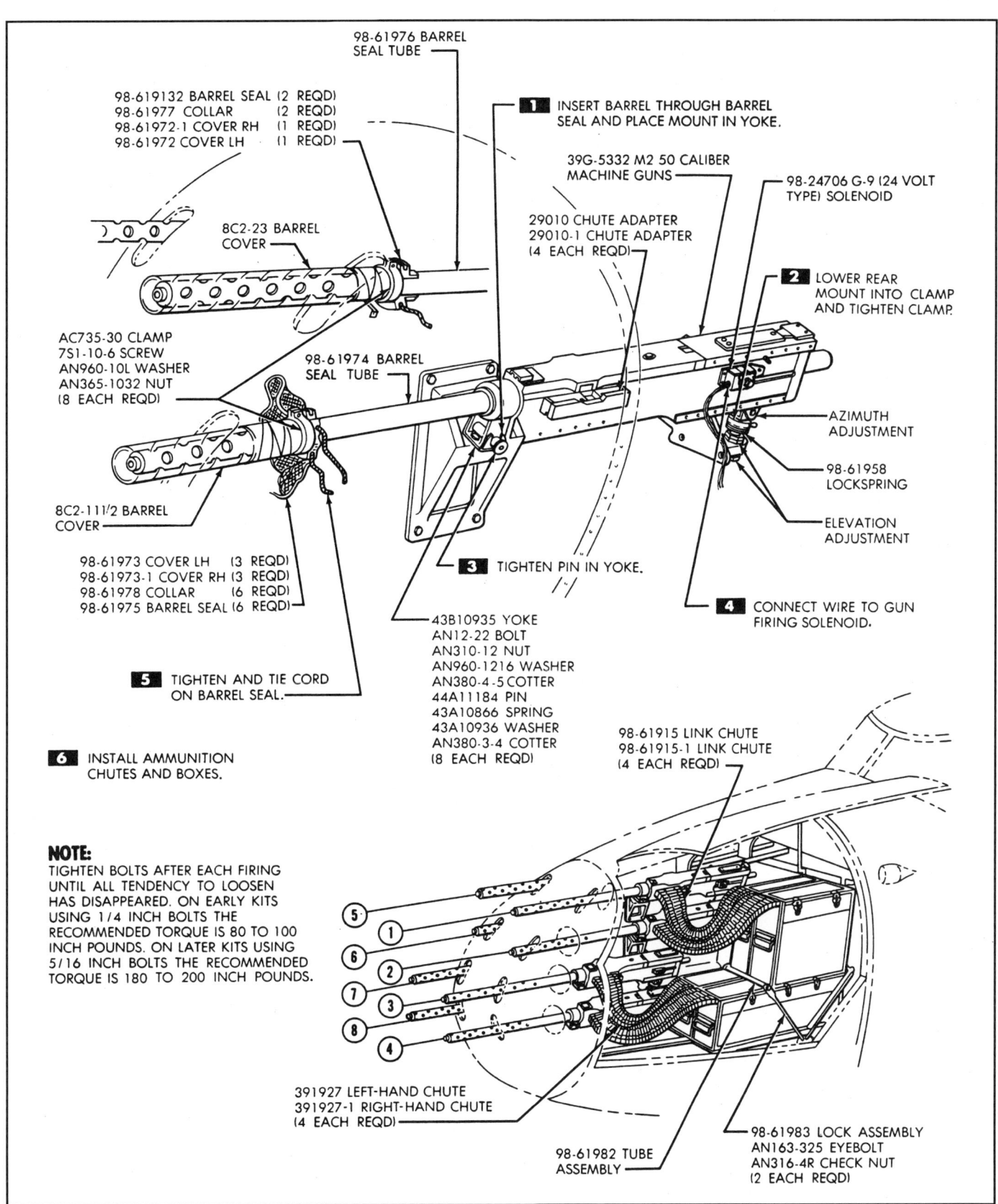

Solid machine gun nose for some B-25Js set four .50-caliber weapons in two bays of four, with the upper four guns staggered farther back than the lower four, as drawn in a B-25J erection and maintenance manual. (Keller/Sturges)

B-25J throttle quadrant between pilot and copilot had paired throttle levers angled toward pilot (near top of photos); propeller pitch levers next to throttles; and fuel mixture knobs angled toward copilot. (NAA)

ing Fortress. The Bendix turret as a ventral emplacement in early B-25s and B-24Ds was considered less than optimum, and often was removed from aircraft in service. A training manual described the version of the lower turret as fitted to the B-25C as weighing about 392 pounds, not counting guns or ammunition. The turret was designed around a central column. "Provisions are made for 390 rounds of ammunition per gun," the manual explained. "Ammunition boxes are bolted to the lower canopy, which can easily be removed from the turret assembly by removing four bolts in the end of the housing hanger arms. Observation windows are provided at each side of the gun turret. The window on the right side of the fuselage just above the floor level is removable and large enough to be used as an emergency escape hatch for the turret operator. The empty cases and links are ejected overboard through a chute at the bottom of the turret."[21]

Bendix ventral turrets used a periscopic gunsight, which, according to training materials, "is tubular in section and is secured within the center column in the exact center of the turret. The eye piece is at the top of the center column and the object prism, which moves in elevation with the guns, is located in the meter box casting at the bottom of the center column. The entire sight rotates in azimuth with the turret." The gunner kneeled at the turret, with padded knee and chest rests helping to keep him in position over the sight optics.[22]

The lower turret's azimuth drive motor served double duty as the retraction and extension power for the turret. When retracted, the turret faired nearly flush with the undersurface of the B-25. Combat operation of the Bendix lower turret in the B-25C consisted of nine steps illuminated in a training manual:

"1. Lower the padded knee support in the radio operator's well forward of the turret.

2. Adjust the chest support as required by means of the spring-loaded pin in the chest support rod.

3. Take kneeling position with the right hand on control handle, left hand on steady grip [a hand rest grip mounted to the turret] and eye on sight eye cushion.

4. The neutral position of the control handle is half-way between the vertical and horizontal rotation stops.

B-25H cockpit set up with control column on pilot's side only. To aid the pilot in sighting targets, an N-3 gunsight with A-1 adjustable sight head was provided. (NAA)

5. To rotate the turret in azimuth, rotate the control handle about its vertical axis. The turret will move in the same relative direction as the handle, at a speed proportional to the degree of control handle rotation.

6. To elevate the guns, rotate the control handle about its horizontal axis. The guns will move in the same relative direction as the handle, at a speed proportional to the degree of control handle rotation.

7. Turn on the windage compensator switch and rotate the rheostat control to indicated airspeed of airplane determined from the pilot. The microphone switch button is located in the end of

A B-25J at Inglewood tested the use of drop tanks. Individual exhaust stack ports are readily evident on engine cowling. (NAA)

B-25 cockpit with single control column shows bow tie control wheel's natural aluminum grips contrasting with black remainder of wheel. Installed N-3 gunsight in photo does not have a sight head attached. (NAA)

the steady grip. The windage compensator on the lower turret is connected to both the upper and lower turret sight.

8. To fire the guns, depress the trigger firing switch in the control handle.

9. Power is cut off by releasing pressure on the dead man switch on the back of the control handle."[23]

The lower turret had electrical limits and dynamic brakes "to prevent mechanical damage to the airplane and also to control the zone of gunfire."[24]

The Bendix Model L upper turret as installed in the B-25C was a twin-.50-caliber electrically operated turret. Each gun could have 440 rounds. Early Bendix upper turrets had a distinct panel for sighting a long tubular gunsight (changed on later models to a more compact optical sight.) The upper turret on the B-25C also had electrical safety mechanism "to prevent firing into the airplane structure except radio antenna and mast." The seated gunner rotated with the turret in azimuth. To rotate the turret, the gunner firmly grasped the control handle with his right hand to depress the dead man switch. Rotating the control handle around its vertical axis caused the turret to move in the same relative direction at a speed proportional to the degree of handle rotation. Elevating the guns was accomplished by rotating the control handle around its horizontal axis. The trigger switch was contained in the control handle. On early top turrets, guns were charged by depressing a

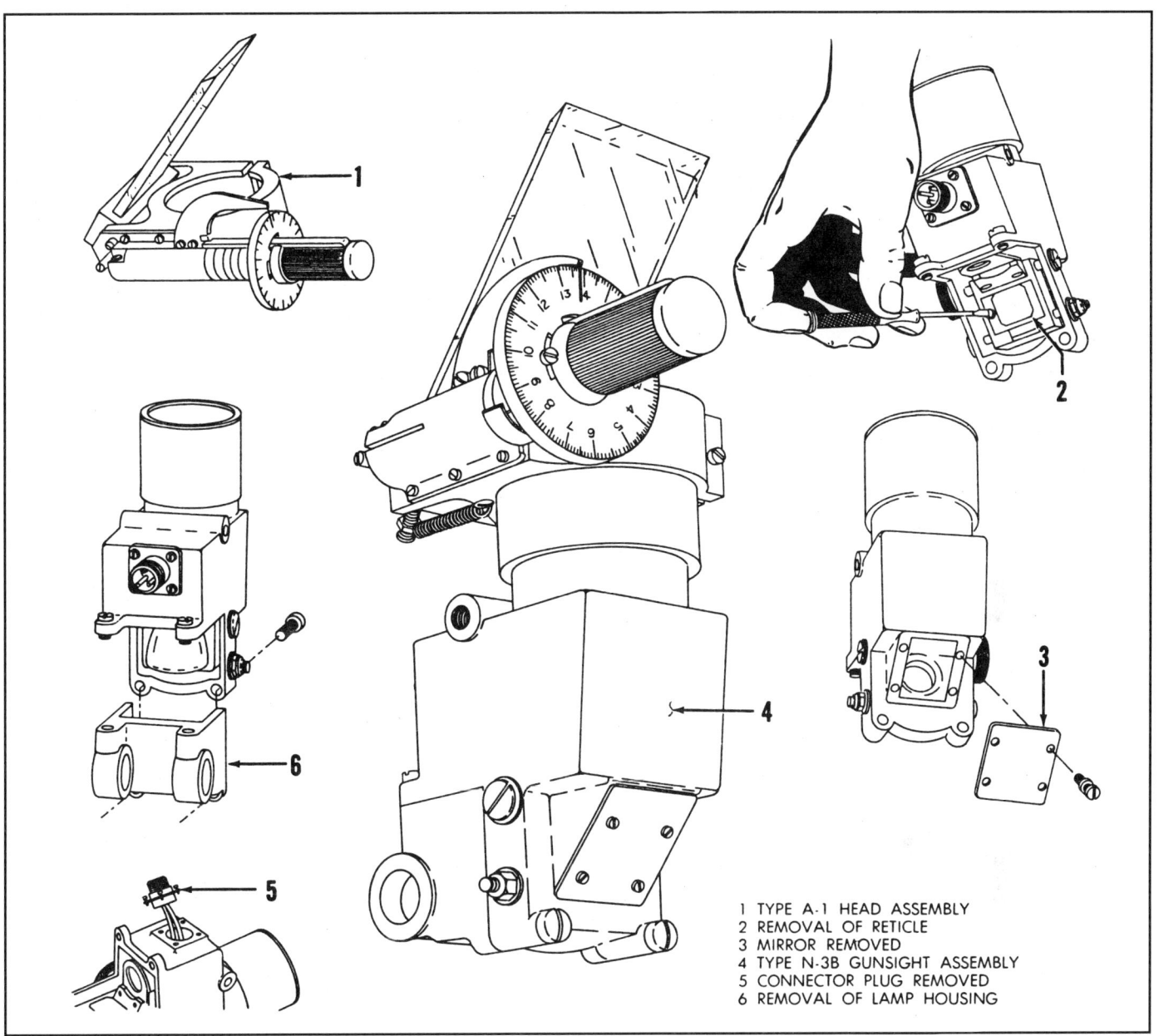

Line art from B-25J erection and maintenance manual depicted N-3B gunsight with A-1 adjustable sight head as used in some Mitchells.

charger button on the left side of the turret's supporting post.[25]

B-25J Armament Described

An Air Force "Dash-1" pilot's manual detailed the aircraft's fixed gun installations: "One fixed .50-caliber machine gun (two on late airplanes) in the nose and four blister guns, two on either side of the forward fuselage, are fired by the pilot. (The flexible nose gun can be converted into a fixed gun fired by the pilot.) For the single nose gun, 300 rounds of ammunition can be carried; when two fixed nose guns are installed, only 275 rounds per gun can be carried. Each blister gun is supplied with 400 rounds of ammunition. All guns may be manually charged in flight." Charging handles for the fixed nose guns were placed on the cockpit floor to the right of the pilot's seat. Charging handles for the blister guns were mounted on the bulkhead at the forward end of the top turret compartment.[26]

The manual said an optical N-3B or N-3C gunsight could be mounted in front of the pilot for sighting the nose and blister guns. Early versions came with an adjustable sighting head that could be used to

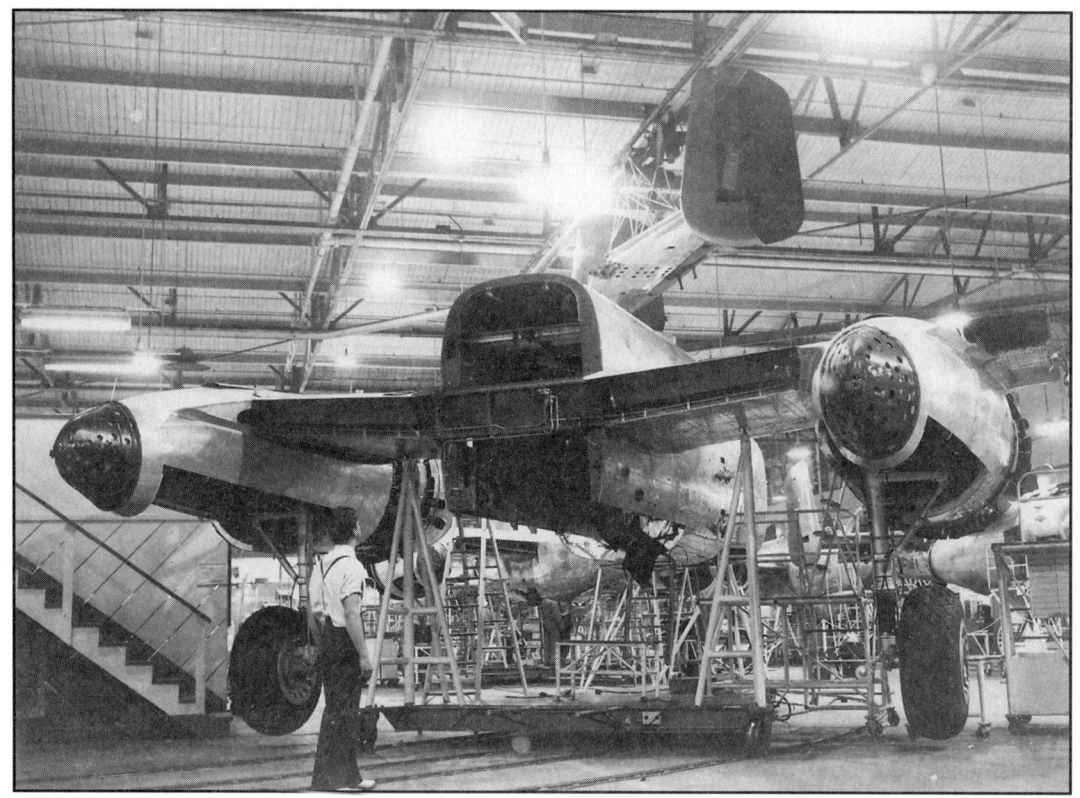

Tracked dollies and trolleys moved B-25 assemblies in cramped quarters at NAA. Assembly break in fuselage coincided with rear of wing box structure. (NAA/Gene Boswell)

aim for low-level bombing attacks as well. Should the electrical gunsight become inoperative, a ring sight was mounted to the right of it, with the corresponding bead sight placed ahead of the windshield. Some B-25s had a gun camera aimed forward through the copilot's windshield.

The B-25J's Bendix top turret was electrically-powered. It was built around a central column that extended up from the floor of the aircraft. Seated on a bicycle-style seat, the gunner moved with the turret as it rotated in azimuth; the guns elevated in slots in the turret's metal-and-Plexiglas dome. Foot rest pedals also served as gun chargers in this Bendix turret. According to the flight manual: "The guns are charged, or a faulty shell removed from the guns, by lifting the footrests to their topmost position and then pushing them down. The left pedal is used to charge the left gun; the right pedal charges the right gun."[27]

The top turret could rotate continuously in azimuth in either direction, and guns could be elevated from the horizontal to straight up. The manual explained: "A gun firing circuit cuts out each gun individually to prevent firing into any part of the airplane. Each gun is supplied with 400 rounds of ammunition. A handcrank is provided for stowing gun and turret in event of electrical power failure." Gunsight was an N-6A optical type.

Two interconnected hand grips controlled speed and direction of movement of the top turret, as detailed in the flight manual: "Twisting the handles left or right rotates the turret horizontally in the related direction. Rotating the handles fore or aft raises or lowers the guns. Rapidity and degree of rotation of the guns and turret are proportional to the speed and degree of movement of the handles from their neutral position. The handles are spring-loaded to neutral when released, and movement of guns or turret is stopped by neutralizing the handles." A safety switch (often informally called a dead man's switch) was mounted in each control handle. If the gunner relaxed his grip, releasing either safety switch, power was interrupted and movement of the turret or guns was stopped. According to the manual: "A trigger is mounted on front of each control handle and will fire the guns whenever the turret main power switch is on."[28]

The electrical power needed to operate the Bendix upper turret was substantial enough to warrant an advisory note in the B-25J flight manual: "When turret is operated on the ground, the engines should be running or an external power source used. Operation of turret on airplane batteries should be kept to an absolute minimum."

Staggered waist windows (the right window was mounted farther forward) each carried one .50-caliber machine gun, to be fired by a crew member identified in the flight manual as the radio operator (a North American Aviation source simply called him the waist gunner). The waist guns were fitted either with ring and bead sights, or with an electric N-8A optical sight. Bell E-11 recoil adapters cradled the flexible waist guns (as well as the flexible nose gun). A combination of rigid and articulated stainless steel ammunition chutes routed ammunition to the waist guns from storage boxes. The flight manual warned: "As there are no fire cutout provisions on waist guns, be careful not to fire into the tail or nacelle."[29]

Hydraulic pressure was key to the use of the Bell boosted tail gun mount in the B-25H and J-models. As described in the pilot's manual, "Pressure for movement of the guns is supplied by two electric pumps: one for horizontal rotation of the guns, the other for raising and lowering them." Early tail gun units relied on an N-8A optical gunsight; later variants could be fitted with a K-10 computing sight. The K-10 could be preset with indicated airspeed and altitude information, from which it could automatically compute "the necessary vertical and lateral deflection angles of the guns for accurate fire." A ring-and-bead sight was fitted for emergency use. Befitting the beleaguered tail gun position, each gun in this emplacement was supplied 600 rounds of ammunition, more than the allotment to other guns aboard the Mitchell.[30]

Two interconnected handles for the tail gun unit operated hydraulic pumps to move the guns. As described in the pilot's manual: "Moving the handles about the horizontal axis rotates the guns in azimuth in the same direction the handles are moved; rotating them fore or aft raises or lowers the guns. The angle of fire is approximately 40 degrees either side of the centerline..." With triggers in both grips, either one could be used to fire the guns. In the event of electrical failure, booster motors which fed ammunition to the tail guns would not work. This necessitated shortening ammunition belts into 75-round lengths that could be fed without the use of booster motors.[31]

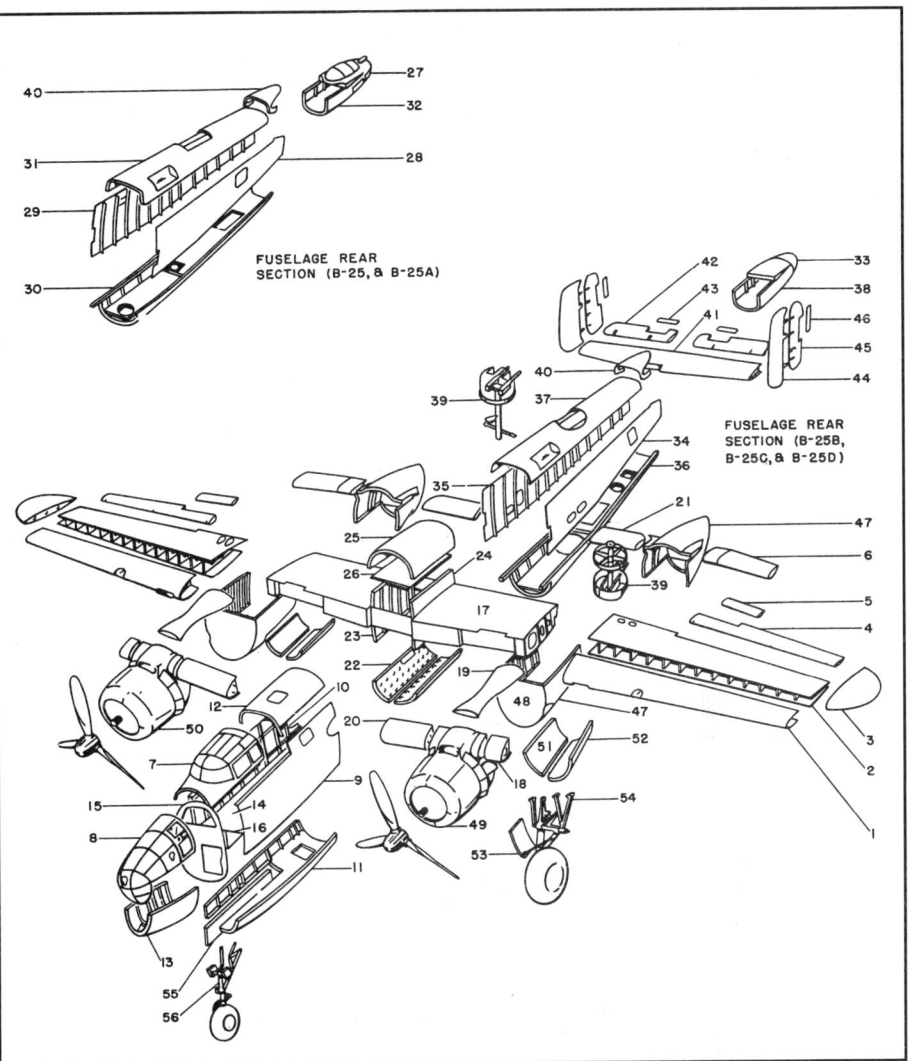

Exploded drawing from B-25 structural repair manual depicted B-25D and earlier versions. (Keller/Sturges)

PICTURE-PERFECT PHOTO MITCHELLS

Modified photo reconnaissance Mitchells, distinguishable by nose camera bulges, were designated F-10s; some wartime trainer B-25s were redesignated AT-24s until subsequently called simply TB-25s. Into the 1950s, Hughes aircraft modified 117 Mitchells to be TB-25Ks and 40 to be TB-25Ms as trainers for the E-1 and E-5 radar fire control systems, respectively. In Alabama, Hayes Aircraft Corp. produced 90 modified TB-25L and 47 TB-25N pilot trainers, the last of which ended this service in the U.S. Air Force in January 1959.[32]

B-25 DELIVERIES AND INVENTORY

B-25 deliveries to the Army Air

Intersection of the curved engine nacelles with the cambered upper surface of the B-25's wing resulted in hourglass shape to top of nacelles. (USAF)

Forces between 1941 and August 1945 totaled 9,816 Mitchells. Of these, only 3,208 came from North American's main plant in Inglewood, California, before B-25 production there ceased in 1943. Beginning with 435 B-25s in 1942, NAA's factory in Kansas City, Kansas, produced 6,608 B-25s. Factory acceptances of B-25s hit an all-time high in May and June 1944 when 396 Mitchells were logged each of those months.[33]

As production methods were streamlined and volumes increased, the average cost of a fly-away complete and armed B-25 decreased from $180,031 in the 1939-41 period to $153,396 in 1942; $151,894 in 1943; $142,194 in 1944; and $116,752 in 1945. Production efficiencies thus overrode the increased costs of more sophisticated hardware and armaments added to the newer Mitchell models.

In December 1941, only 151 B-25s were in the Army Air Forces inventory. At the end of April, 1942 (the month Jimmy Doolittle used 16 B-25Bs on what became a one-way mission over Tokyo) 260 Mitchells were tallied in the AAF. By December 1942, 1,128 Mitchells were in the Air Force. All-time high level of B-25s in the Army Air Forces was achieved by the end of July 1944, when 2,656 first-line Mitchells were inventoried by the service. By August 1945, this tally was 1,865 first-line B-25s.[34]

A contract log maintained by NAA used the nomenclature NA-62 to cover B-25s, B-25As and B-25Bs ordered under one contract in 1939. Serial numbers began with 40-2165 and ended with 40-2348; number 40-2174 was the first Mitchell to have gull wings. NA-82 was applied to a B-25C contract of 1940, covering aircraft from serial 41-12434 to 41-13296. NA-87 represented B-25D-1, -5, -10, and -15 blocks with serials from 41-29648 to 41-30847 made in Kansas. NA-90 was assigned to a June 1941 contract for B-25C-5 aircraft built at Inglewood, and intended for the Netherlands.

In addition to Netherlands serials, these aircraft were allocated USAAF numbers 42-53332 through 42-53493. NA-93 applied to 150 B-25Cs built at Inglewood as Defense Aid for China; they were allocated USAAF serials 42-32383 through

42-32532, according to the NAA airframe contract record.[35]

NA-94 applied to a 150-aircraft batch that included the one B-25E heated-wing experimental aircraft (42-32281) along with B-25C-10s intended as Defense Aid for Britain, and given USAAF serials 42-32233 through 42-32382 (less the B-25E). NA-96 was the NAA charge number for a March 1942 contract for B-25C-20 and -25 Mitchells totaling 300 aircraft, built at Inglewood with serials 42-64502 through 42-64801; NA-96 also applied to 400 B-25G-5 and -10 aircraft with serials 42-64802 through 42-64901, and 42-64902 through 65201. The NAA charge number NA-98 was assigned in mid-1942 to a contract for 1,000 B-25Hs with USAAF serials 43-4105 through 5104, built at Inglewood. One of this batch (43-1406) was fitted with R-2800 engines; it later crashed. NA-100 was the company charge number for an order of B-25D-20, -25, -30, and -35 Mitchells built at Kansas City, with USAAF serials 42-87113 to 42-87312; 42-87313 to 42-87612; and 43-3280 to 43-3869.[36]

NA-108 represented a contract for B-25J-1, -5, -10, -15, -20, -25, -30, and -35 Mitchells totaling more than 4,300 aircraft from the Kansas City plant. Serials 43-3870 to 43-4069 and 43-4070 to 43-4104 were aircraft transferred from charge number NA-100. Serials 43-27473 to 43-28222 and 43-35946 to 43-36245 were aircraft transferred from charge number NA-114. The huge size of charge order NA-108 enveloped vast blocks of serial numbers of B-25Js including 44-28711 to 44-31110; 44-31111 to 44-31510; 44-86692 to 44-86897; 45-8801 to 45-8818; 45-8820 to 45-8823; 45-8825 to 45-8828; and 44-8832 (as it appears on the NAA record; this may be a typographical error that should read 45-8832). Seventy-two B-25Js of this batch,

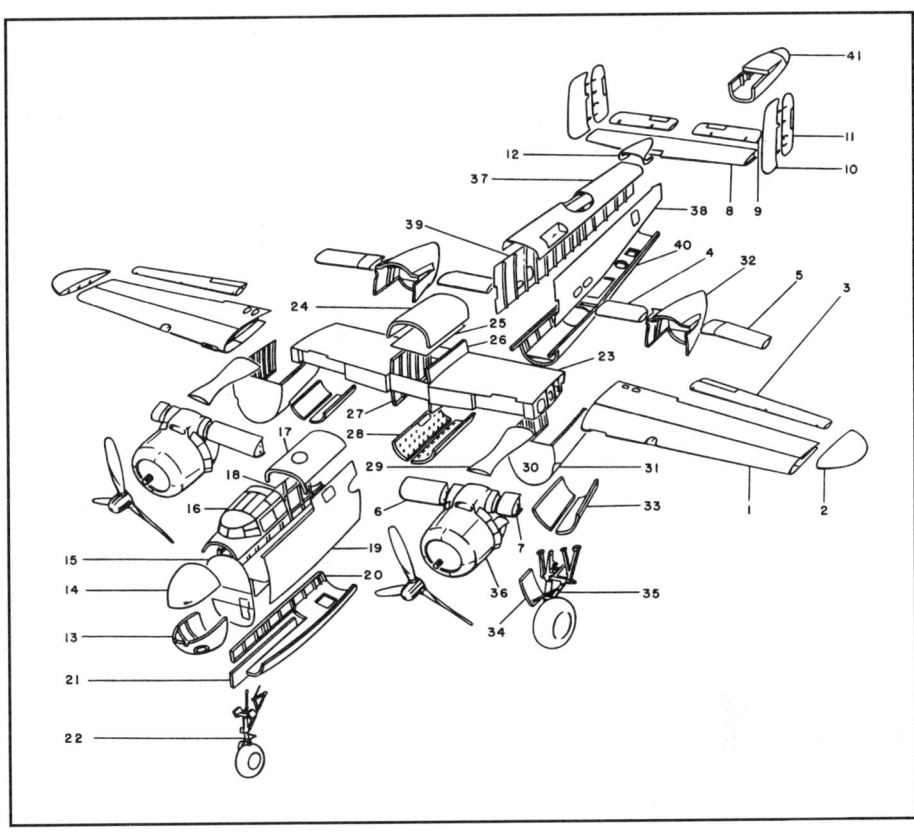

B-25G exploded view showed short nose with provision for 75MM cannon (not shown). (Keller/Sturges)

although in flyable condition, were not completed and accepted contractually. They were part of the termination inventory at the end of B-25 production. Their serial numbers were 45-8819; 45-8824; 45-8829 to 45-8831; and 45-8833 to 45-8899.[37]

Canceled orders for B-25s at one time carried NAA charge numbers including NA-113 intended for B-25Hs; NA-114 and NA-115 (B-25Js transferred to NA-108).[38]

[1] News Release, "The Story of the B-25 Mitchell," North American Aviation, Inc., Jan 1963. [2] Peter M. Bowers and Gordon Swanborough, *United States Military Aircraft Since 1908*, Putnam, London, 1971. [3] From 50th anniversary reunion banquet sponsored by Kirsten Wind Tunnel, University of Washington, 1988. [4] From "Airplane Three-view Dimensions — B-25H" in USAAF B-25 structural repair manual AN 01-60G-3. [5] "Design Analysis of The North American B-25 Mitchell," by C.J. Hansen, NAA chief project engineer, *Aviation*, March 1945. [6] Discussion, author with former Northwest Airlines employee Robert Nielson, circa 1969. (Nielson recalled stamping his initials —RN — in the wooden dummy barrels at the time.) [7] "Design Analysis of The North American B-25 Mitchell," by C.J. Hansen, NAA chief project engineer, *Aviation*, March 1945. [8] Discussion, author with B-25 restorer Tony Ritzman, 8 March 1997. [9] Peter M. Bowers and Gordon Swanborough, *United States Military Aircraft Since 1908*, Putnam, London, 1971. [10] Monthly Chart, *Armament and Bomb Installations*, AAF Aircraft, Engineering Division, Air Technical Service Command, Wright Field, Ohio, 1 August 1945. [11] Ibid. [12] Ibid. [13] Ibid. [14] Ibid. [15] Ibid. [16] Ibid. [17] Gun Install. Lecture — B-25 Series Airplanes, NAA Field Service Department, 15 September 1942. [18] Ibid. [19] Ibid. [20] Ibid. [21] Ibid. [22] Ibid. [23] Ibid. [24] Ibid. [25] Ibid. [26] From postwar edition of USAF B-25J flight manual (AN 01-60GE-1). [27] Ibid. [28] Ibid. [29] Ibid. [30] Ibid. [31] Ibid. [32] Peter M. Bowers and Gordon Swanborough, *United States Military Aircraft Since 1908*, Putnam, London, 1971. [33] Army Air Forces Statistical Digest — World War II, USAAF Office of Statistical Control, December 1945. [34] Ibid. [35] Excerpt from NAA Airframe Contract Record as of 3/20/57. [36] Ibid. [37] Ibid. [38] Ibid.

ICONS OVER TOKYO

DOOLITTLE RAID ASSURED B-25'S PLACE IN HISTORY

The B-25's service was punctuated early in the war by the unorthodox launching of 16 B-25s from the aircraft carrier USS Hornet to bomb targets around Tokyo, Yokohama, Kobe, and Nagoya on 18 April 1942. As early as 6 April, 10 DC-3 airliners belonging to Pan American Airways began carrying 30,000 gallons of aviation gasoline and 500 gallons of lubricants from Calcutta, India, to an airstrip at Asansol, for further carriage into China, where it was intended to use these petroleum products to enable Doolittle's raiders to fly after their arrival in China. The Doolittle B-25s were launched earlier than planned, farther out to sea, after their location might have been compromised by a Japanese vessel that was subsequently sunk.[1]

This additional distance to the target meant the B-25s would not have enough fuel to reach their intended Chinese landing fields. Instead, 15 of the Mitchells made crash landings or were abandoned in China; one of the B-25s landed near Vladivostok, where it and its crew were interned by edgy Soviets. (At the time, the Soviet Union was not at war with Japan, and some Soviets feared Japan would open a second front against them if it appeared the Soviets cooperated with the Doolittle raid.)

Carrying wooden dowels to mimic tail guns, Doolittle's 16 B-25Bs were part of a contingent built without any real tail armament, based on the belief that dorsal and ventral power turrets would adequately protect the bombers. The remotely-sighted Bendix ventral turrets also were deleted from Doolittle's B-25 force to allow for additional gasoline tankage. The Doolittle B-25s received modifications at the Northwest Orient Airlines center in St. Paul, Minnesota, to increase their gasoline capacity, followed by more alterations and performance tuneups at McClellan Field's Sacramento Air Depot, in California, before being loaded aboard the USS Hornet for the sea trip toward Japan.

Some of the McClellan mechanics later described Doolittle's aircrews as anxious and almost interfering with the work being done on their Mitchells; security precautions kept the mechanics in the dark about the nature of the Doolittle operation. Had the Sacramento Air Depot workers understood the high danger of the enterprise they were assisting, the attitudes of some of the more protective members of the Doolittle mission would have been understandable.[2]

Following a six-day stint at Sacramento, the Doolittle B-25s were flown to Alameda, California, to be hoisted aboard the aircraft carrier Hornet. Years later Adm. James Russell, who in 1942 commanded a force of PBY Catalinas in the Aleutians, recalled a flight he made over Alameda as the Doolittle Mitchells were being loaded on the Hornet's deck with as much secrecy as such a process would permit. Admiral Russell said at the time he saw the aircraft carrier's flight deck choked with Army B-25s he thought it was a terrible waste of naval aviation to use an aircraft carrier to ferry USAAF bombers overseas. Only after the raid did Russell learn that he had witnessed no mere shipment of bombers to the front; he had looked down upon a most profound wedding of the Air Force and the Navy to strike a blow as soon as possible to the heart of Japan.[3]

The successful launching of all 16 B-25s, and their subsequent bombing of Japan, rightly earned respect for Doolittle and his crews, who showed enterprise and confidence, the hallmarks of Yankee ingenuity that did so much to win World War Two.

In the benchmark books, *The Army Air Forces in World War II*, edited by W.F. Craven and J.L. Cate, credence is given to the popular notion that the Doolittle Tokyo raid had morale-boosting as a core goal right from the start, when it was conceived in January 1942. A seaborne air strike against Tokyo was a good way to boost Allied spirits and at the same time send a chilling message to the Japanese high command that their homeland was not inviolate. In fact, while the actual bombing did have some direct consequences against a variety of targets, this was but a token compared with the greater impact the Doolittle mission had on American society and Japanese defense planners. The Japanese felt compelled, after the attack, to retain four army fighter groups at home instead of committing them to the

Solomon Islands, where they were badly needed in 1942 and 1943. Additionally, the raid may have pushed the Japanese into expanding their forays into Midway and the Aleutians, which ultimately cost the Japanese navy the cream of its carrier aviation assets in the rout at Midway in early June 1942.[4]

When the raid was planned, it was assumed the bombers would launch from the aircraft carrier close enough to the Japanese homeland to ensure the raiders the range needed to fly about 1,200 miles farther west to land at airfields in China. Using gasoline secreted there ahead of time, the raiders would move on to Chungking and thence into the stream of American combat aircraft in the far east.

To lead this ambitious undertaking, Gen. Henry H. "Hap" Arnold chose Lt. Col. James H. Doolittle, whose flying acumen was already legendary. Doolittle and the planners evaluated several twin engine bombers as candidates for this unorthodox mission. The B-18 and B-23 were ruled out, as was the Martin B-26. North American's B-25 Mitchell seemed to fit the requirement, although the Doolittle airplanes would require additional fuel tanks and other modifications. With the selection of the B-25, it made sense to cultivate experienced Mitchell crews for the risky mission. Colonel Doolittle asked for volunteers from the 17th Bomb Group, the unit which had received the first operational B-25s back at McChord Field, Washington, the previous year.

So crucial was the need for extended range, even after extra fuel tanks were installed, the B-25Bs of the

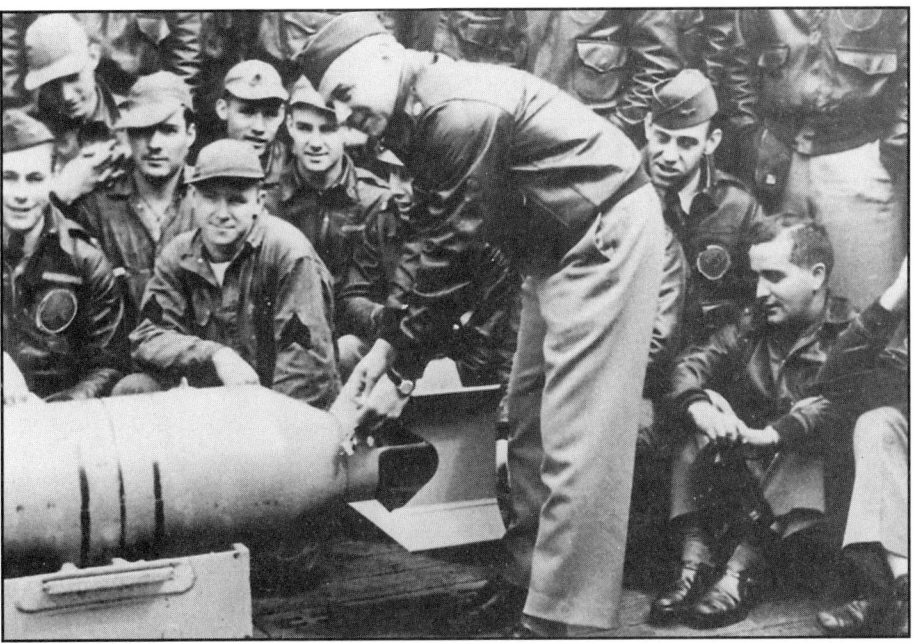

Then-Lt. Col. Jimmy Doolittle attached a prewar Japanese medal to a bomb aboard the USS Hornet to return the medal during the mission he led over Tokyo 18 April 1942.

Doolittle mission each carried 10 five-gallon gasoline cans, the contents of which were emptied into the fuel tanks as gasoline was burned off in flight. A rubber bladder carrying 160 gallons was stashed in the crawlspace of each bomber, raising the total gasoline tankage to 1,141 gallons per aircraft, of which 1,100 was considered usable.

With an all-up weight of 31,000 pounds, the gasoline- and bomb-laden B-25Bs of the Doolittle mission would be expected to get airborne from the crowded wooden flight deck of an aircraft carrier, with a deck run of only 467 feet, to start clear of the conning tower. The B-25s were too large to stow below deck. Early practice in Florida under the guidance of Navy Lt. Henry F. Miller showed the B-25 pilots they could leave a paved runway in 700 to 750 feet. At sea, with the aircraft carrier steaming full speed into the wind, the bombers would gain airspeed from these combined sources of headwind, effectively shortening their takeoff runs. Yet this was not an ordinary thing to do with a heavily loaded twin-engine bomber; it was fraught with danger and the need for careful timing and precision under even the most ideal of conditions.

Rather than risk Norden bombsights over Japan, the raiders left these precision devices behind, using instead an ingeniously simple mechanical sight devised by Capt. C. Ross Greening, a clever and artistic member of the team. Training included bombing practice from about 1,500 feet. Run-in to the target at minimum altitude was followed by a pull-up to bombing altitude, to minimize exposing the B-25s to enemy gunners.[5]

By 24 March 1942, the crews were ordered to fly their special B-25s to Alameda Naval Air Station, near San Francisco, by way of McClellan

Army Air Base for last-minute adjustments.

Ultimately 16 B-25s were loaded aboard the USS Hornet at Alameda on 1 April. On the following day, the Hornet, two cruisers, four destroyers, and an oiler, slipped past the Golden Gate bridge. North of Midway, a force of similar composition (but without additional B-25s) joined the Hornet, doubling the size of the surface fleet heading toward Japan. Rough seas characterized the voyage. In his planning, Doolittle wanted to get within 450 miles of Japan before launching from the aircraft carrier, but he thought the launch could be made from a distance of 550 miles if detection by the Japanese warranted this. The United States could ill afford to lose the task force in combat close to Japan.

Early the morning of 18 April 1942, the task force encountered a Japanese picket boat. Certain the force's secrecy was now compromised, Doolittle faced a difficult, albeit already contemplated, choice. His bombers would make a flight of 800 miles to Japan if they launched now; if they delayed, the task force's safety would be jeopardized. The decision was made to launch from this greater distance, and hope to make some kind of safe landfall in China.

Less than an hour after the picket boat was sighted, Doolittle made good his takeoff from the Hornet at 8:18 a.m. local time. A 40-knot gale actually aided the B-25s, although heavy seas plunged water over the aircraft carrier's deck, making it desirable to time the takeoff runs to reach the end of the deck as it was high on a swell instead of down in a trough. The last of 16 B-25s successfully launched by 9:21 that morning, some dipping perilously close to the sea as they labored to achieve altitude.

Japanese intelligence presumed no aircraft could possibly reach Japan from such a range as their picket ship reported; therefore, no raid was expected on the 18th of April, to the benefit of the B-25 crews. Fifteen minutes after noon on 18 April 1942, Colonel Doolittle dropped bombs over Tokyo, followed by the 15 other raiders roaring low over several key Japanese cities. A claim was made for one bomb from Lt. Edgar McElroy's Mitchell hitting the dry-docked aircraft carrier Ryuho at the Yokosuka naval base. Only one of the B-25s received any anti-aircraft hits, and damage was slight to this aircraft.[6]

All 16 B-25s exited Japan intact, heading toward China. An unexpected tailwind helped the raiders as they flew across the East China Sea toward a landing field at Chuchow. Clouds, rain, and nightfall intervened to deny any of the raiders a chance to find the landing field if fuel starvation didn't end their flights first. Some crews elected to bail out; others rode their Mitchells down to forced landings along the coast of China. Forty-nine of 50 raiders who bailed out landed safely; 10 more in two B-25s survived forced landings, although some were injured seriously.[7]

The crew of one of the bombers, B-25B number 40-2242, piloted by Capt. Edward J. York, landed near Vladivostok, Russia, to the consternation of the Soviets who were not yet at war with Japan. York's crew was interned and their B-25 was impounded.[8] Tantalizing stories persisted long after the war that this historic Doolittle raider B-25B survived intact in the Soviet Union; as of this writing, efforts are underway by dedicated researcher Walter Kurilchyk and his Russian contacts to penetrate decades of Soviet records in a search for B-25 number 40-2242.

The Mitchells flown by lieutenants Dean Hallmark and William Farrow came to earth in Japanese-held territory. Two men in Hallmark's crew evidently drowned in their bomber when it ditched; another died in Japanese prison in 1943. Three of Doolittle's raiders, lieutenants Farrow, Hallmark, and Sgt. Harold Spatz, were executed by the Japanese on 15 October 1942 after a trial; four other raiders were kept prisoner until the end of the war.

The Doolittle raid on Tokyo will live in the annals of warfare as a remarkable feat for successfully launching loaded medium bombers from an aircraft carrier for a combat mission. It will live on in history also for the plucky, and yet typical, young American men who pulled it off in the face of daunting odds, led by a modestly savvy lieutenant colonel in a bomber named for an Air Corps firebrand of a previous era.

[1] Kit C. Carter and Robert Mueller, compilers, *Combat Chronology 1941-1945 — U.S. Army Air Forces in World War II*, Center for Air Force History, Washington, DC, 1991. [2] Ben Warner, "Six Days," *American Aviation Historical Society Journal*, Spring 1994, Pp. 68-74. [3] From comments made by Adm. James Russell during a reunion of Doolittle's Raiders in Tacoma, Wash., in 1989. [4] W.F. Craven and J.L. Cate, editors, *The Army Air Forces in World War II*, Vol. 1, Office of Air Force History imprint, Washington, DC, 1983; originally published by the University of Chicago, 1948. [5] *Ibid*. [6] *Ibid*. [7] *Ibid*. [8] Stan Cohen, *Destination: Tokyo — A Pictorial History of Doolittle's Tokyo Raid, April 18, 1942*, Pictorial Histories Publishing Co., Missoula, Montana, 1983.

THE B-25 GOES TO WAR

USAAF MITCHELLS AROUND THE WORLD

B-25s entered combat in 1942. The following highlights from B-25 operations serve to illustrate the Mitchell's wartime USAAF service. It is possible some entries represent multiple sorties by the same aircraft on a given day. Some events in this combat listing are representative; others are unusual. Combined, they provide a quick overview of the B-25 at war. While the Doolittle raid on Tokyo on 18 April 1942 raised the B-25 to almost legendary status, the Mitchell's war was frequently spectacular on a daily basis around the world.

On 10 May 1942, Fifth Air Force dispatched B-25s to bomb a Japanese seaplane base at Deboyne Island. On 14 May, Mitchells of the Fifth AF were part of a menu of bombers launched to strike targets including Lae and Rabaul; two days later they

Natural metal finish on B-25Js highlights raised "doghouse" tail gunner's position, necessitating armor plates aft of dorsal turret gun muzzles to protect tail gunner from accidental cook-off rounds. Some J-models — especially those sent to the MTO — deleted the package guns depicted in these examples. (NAA and Gene Furnish)

Waist guns in B-25H and J-models were slightly staggered; some Mitchell crews carried only one waist gunner to man both weapons. E-11 recoil adapters in photo are fitted with N-8 gunsights. (NAA)

Size of the angular B-25 vertical stabilizer and rudder is apparent from the height of a mechanic standing beside an oil-spattered 12th Bomb Group example. (12th Bomb Group Association)

again targeted Lae and the Deboyne seaplane base. (Air Force chronology entries sometimes group several types of bombers and several targets for a single day's activities for a particular numbered air force; it is possible B-25s hit only some of the specified targets for a given day.) Tenth Air Force's early use of B-25s was dogged by disaster on 3 June 1942 when a flight of six 11th Bomb Squadron B-25s, intended for the China Air Task Force, left Dinjan for China. On the way to Kunming, the Mitchells dropped bombs on Lashio; after this, three of the force crashed into a mountain hidden by overcast. A fourth B-25 of the small 10th AF contingent was abandoned near Chan-i as it ran out of gasoline; the two surviving Mitchells reached Kunming, one bearing a dead radio operator as the result of a fighter attack. During June, Fifth Air Force B-25s continued hitting Japanese targets occasionally, as on the last day of that month when B-25s and B-26s hit Lae, New Guinea.[1]

On 1 July 1942, three days before its formal activation, the first combat mission of the China Air Task Force (CATF), not counting the dis-

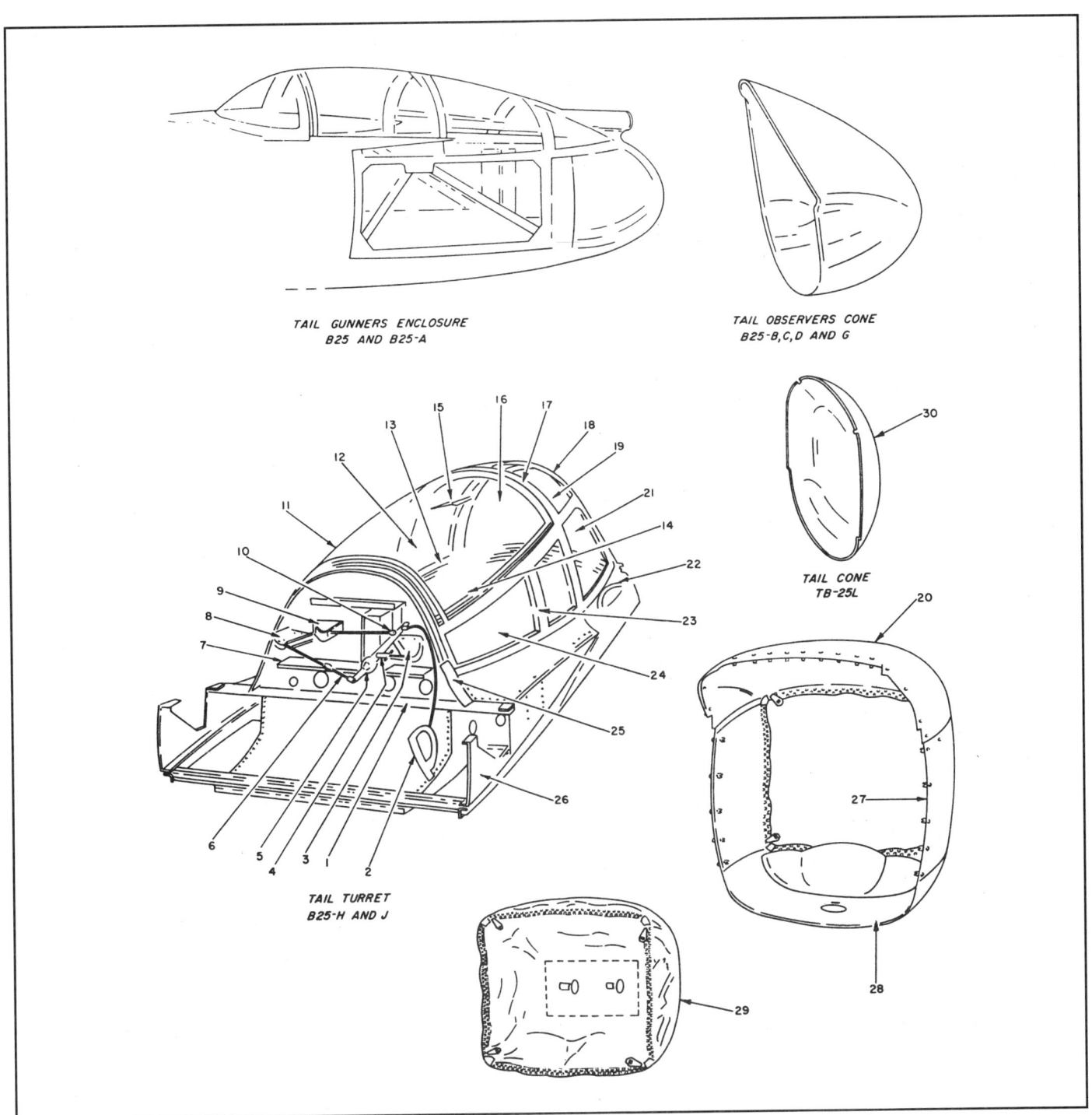

B-25 structural repair manual shows various tail-end configurations. Some (B-25, B-25A, B-25H, and B-25J) were armed emplacements. Tail observer's cone for models B through G left the factory unarmed, although many field modifications saw a variety of .30-caliber and .50-caliber mounts installed in these aircraft. (Carl Scholl/Aero Trader)

astrous 3 June delivery mission, saw four B-25s from Hengyang, escorted by P-40s, bomb docks at Hankow. Bad weather handicapped the mission, and results were of little consequence. Next day, the CATF B-25s and P-40s returned to Hankow's docks, registering more damage this time. Col. Caleb V. Haynes, commander of CATF bombers, flew a single-ship B-25 mission on 8 July to drop bombs on a Japanese headquarters at Tengchung, near the Burma border. In response to a Chinese request, on 19 July a pair of CATF B-25s attacked Japanese troops at Linchwan, breaking a stalemate and

allowing Chinese forces to enter the city the following day.[2]

By the end of July 1942, the 12th Bomb Group was bringing B-25s into Palestine. Tenth AF B-25s claimed two Japanese interceptors shot down during an 8 August strike in the Canton vicinity. The first CATF raid over Indochina happened the following day when four B-25s and three P-40s, staging through Nanning, bombed warehouses and docks at Haiphong, claiming a freighter sunk. The debut of the 12th Bomb Group in the middle east came on 17 August 1942 when B-25s of the 81st Bomb Squadron attacked a tank repair area, stores, and a depot at Matruh. Middle east B-25s again attacked Matruh on 22 August, when the new American bombers caused confusion for the crew of a RAF Beaufighter, which mistakenly shot down one of the Mitchells. (Possibly as a result of incidents like this, B-25s of the 12th Bomb Group adopt-

B-25 Bendix top turret dome was reinforced with three clear Plexiglas strips. Aluminum fairings on top of fuselage were streamlining for angled steel armor deflector plates that shielded tail gunner from accidental firings of the top turret. In service, some B-25s flew with the fairings removed, exposing the bare armor plates. (Rockwell International/Gene Boswell)

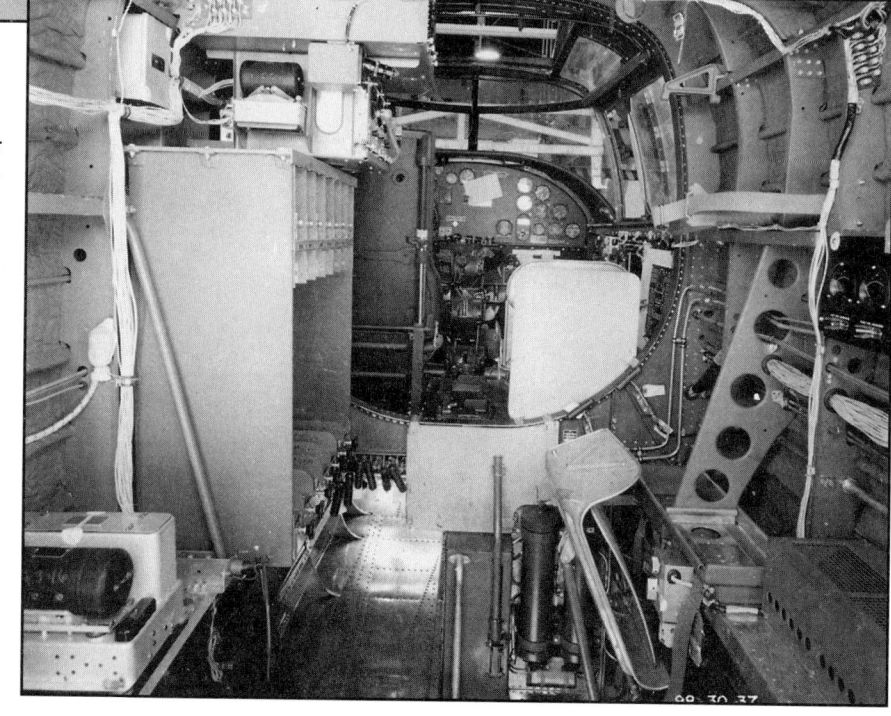

Photo looking forward in cannon-armed B-25 shows ammunition storage rack for 75MM rounds at left. At 5-O'clock position on rounded bulkhead are charging handles for righthand package guns. Quilted insulation lined the inside of the fuselage. (NAA)

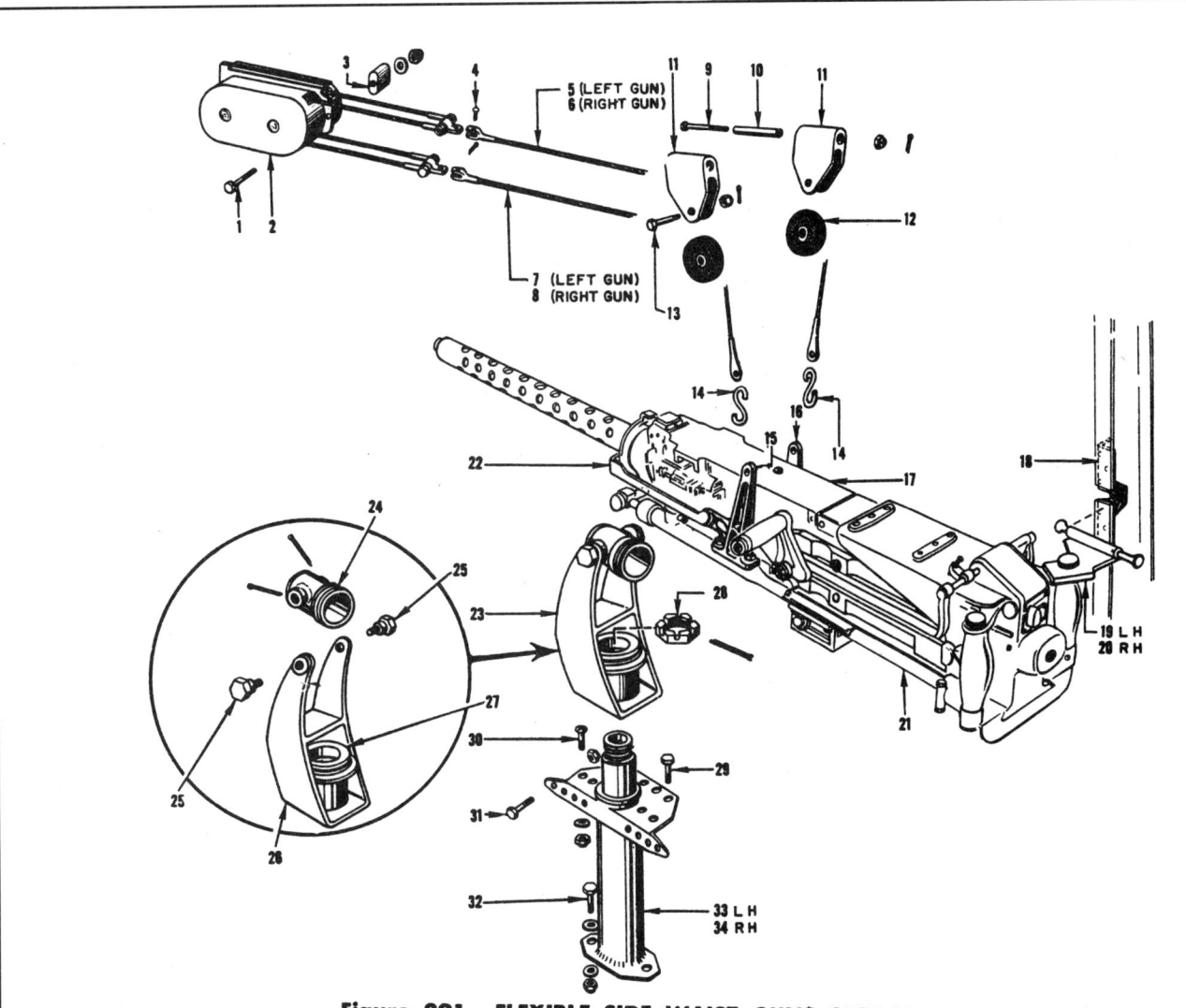

Figure 291 FLEXIBLE SIDE WAIST GUNS SUPPORTS

ARMAMENT GROUP
FLEXIBLE SIDE WAIST GUNS SUPPORT

Figure & Index Number	PART NUMBER	NOMENCLATURE	USAGE CODE	UNITS PER ASSY
291-4	AN393-7	Pin—Flat head 3/16	All	2
291-5	98-62547-5	Cable Assy—Flexible .50 caliber side waist gun bungee (Left upper inboard at bungee)	A	1
	98-62547-12	Cable Assy—Flexible .50 caliber side waist gun bungee (Left upper inboard at bungee)	B-C, J	1
291-6	98-62547-3	Cable Assy—Flexible .50 caliber side waist gun bungee (Right upper inboard at bungee)	All	1
291-7	98-62547-4	Cable Assy—Flexible .50 caliber side waist gun bungee (Left lower outboard at bungee)	A	1
	98-62547-10	Cable Assy—Flexible .50 caliber side waist gun bungee (Left lower outboard at bungee)	B-C, J	1
291-8	98-62547-2	Cable Assy—Flexible .50 caliber side waist gun bungee (Right lower outboard at bungee)	All	1
291-9	AN3-30	Bolt—Aircraft, #10-32	All	2
	AN310-3	Nut—Aircraft castle	All	2
291-10	4B14-3-80	Bushing—Spacer	All	2
291-11	98-62556	Support—Flexible .50 caliber side waist gun bungee pulley	All	2
291-12	AN210-2A	Pulley—Anti friction bearing control	All	2
291-13	AN3-10	Bolt—Aircraft, #10-32	All	2
	AN310-3	Nut—Aircraft castle	All	2
291-14	98-62539	Link—Flexible .50 caliber side waist gun bungee cable attaching	All	2
291-15	98-62505	Bracket—Flexible .50 caliber side waist gun bungee LH (See figure 290-19)	All	Ref
291-16	98-62505-1	Bracket—Flexible .50 caliber side waist gun bungee RH (See figure 290-18)	All	Ref
291-17	M2	Gun—Machine, caliber .50, Browning, M2, aircraft, basic (GFE) (See figure 290-14)	All	Ref

Waist gun mount on H and J-model Mitchells used specialized E-11 recoil adapter with balancing cable system and a swiveling yoke, as drawn for a "Dash-4" illustrated parts book. (Bill Miranda collection)

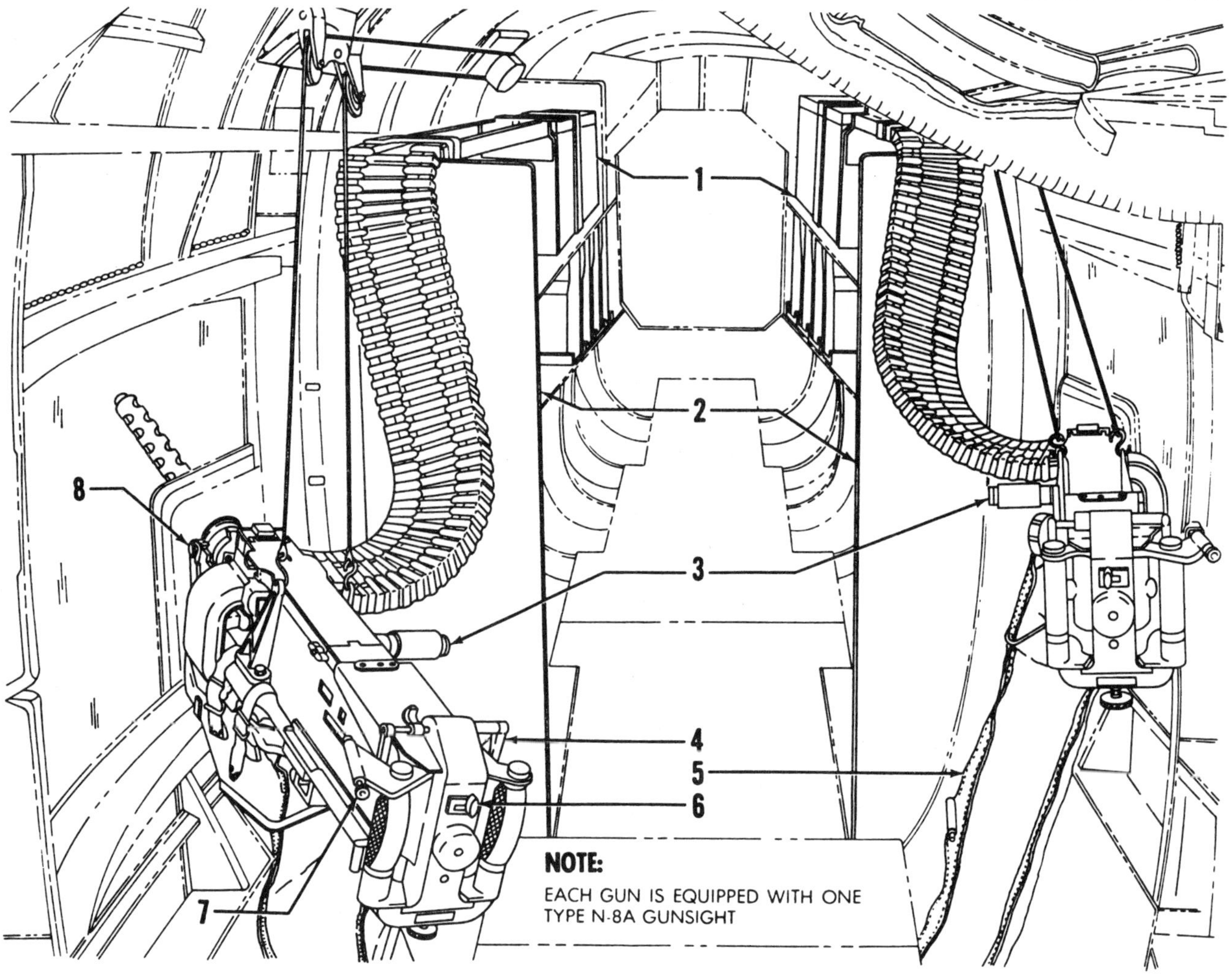

```
1  AMMUNITION BOXES         4  TRIGGER                      7  STOWAGE PLUNGER
2  1/4 INCH ARMOR PLATE     5  CASE AND LINK EJECTION BAG   8  GUN ADAPTER LATCH
3  CHARGING HANDLES         6  SAFETY
```

NOTE: EACH GUN IS EQUIPPED WITH ONE TYPE N-8A GUNSIGHT

Figure 11-84. Waist Gun Installation

B-25H and J waist gun detail drawing showed use of flexible and rigid ammunition feed chutes from ammo boxes mounted aft of the guns. (Keller/Sturges)

ed British-recommended recognition markings in north Africa, including RAF-style fin flashes on both sides of their twin vertical fins. Some flew with U.S. national insignia on both wings instead of staggered on upper left and lower right.)[3]

In the late summer of 1942, General George Kenney's Fifth Air Force Mitchells were consuming spare parts and suffering at the end of a long supply pipeline. With several B-25s grounded in New Guinea for want of spare parts including wheel bearings, daring and imaginative maintenance men and airmen came together with a plan. A downed B-25 near Bena Bena had not burned, and might be a cornucopia of parts for the other Mitchells on New Guinea. A transport crew was willing to fly a DC-3 to a small strip near the site, but nobody knew for certain if reputed cannibals in the region were pro-Allied or pro-Japanese, or if Japanese patrols might reach the area. A sergeant and three mechanics were let off at Bena Bena by the DC-3 crew who returned four days later to ferry the men and their incredible cache of B-25 parts out. Assisted by a train of friendly natives, the men packed out most of the B-25

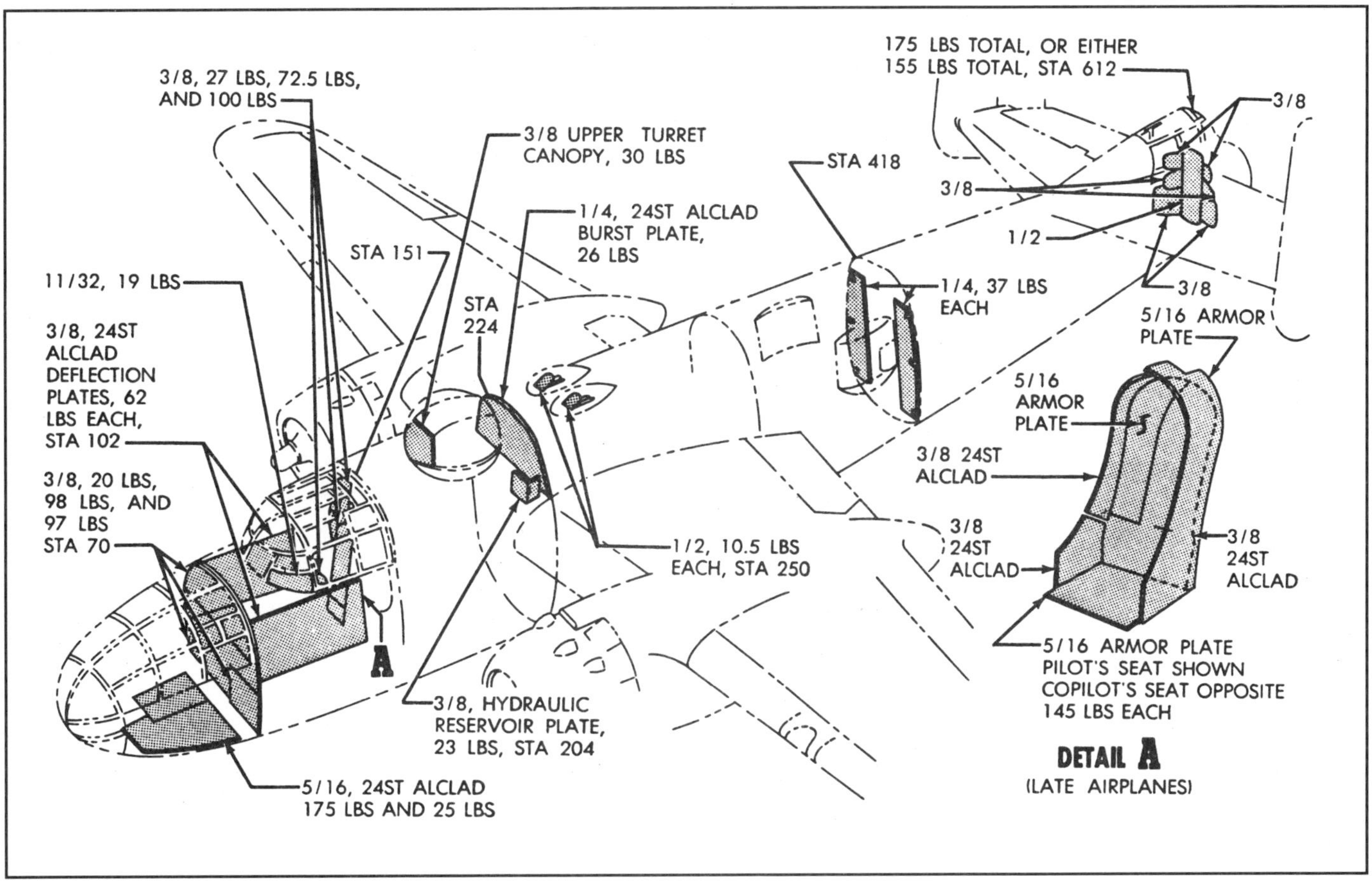

Armor plate was depicted in the B-25J erection and maintenance manual. So-called "coffin seats" enclosed pilot and copilot in armor. (Keller/Sturges collection)

as well as a P-39 wreck they found nearby. The number of in-commission aircraft at port Moresby rose as a direct result of this early-day recycling of parts.[4]

On 28 August 1942, CATF's largest medium-bomber mission to date saw eight unescorted B-25s attack ammo dumps and barracks at Hoang Su Phi and a fuel dump at Phu Lo. As the autumn of 1942 approached, USAAF B-25 operations overseas emphasized China, the middle east, and Fifth Air Force in the south Pacific. The first Ameri-

Starting life as B-25D-10-NC number 43-130181, this Mitchell became a bug-eyed F-10 camera platform. (Bowers collection)

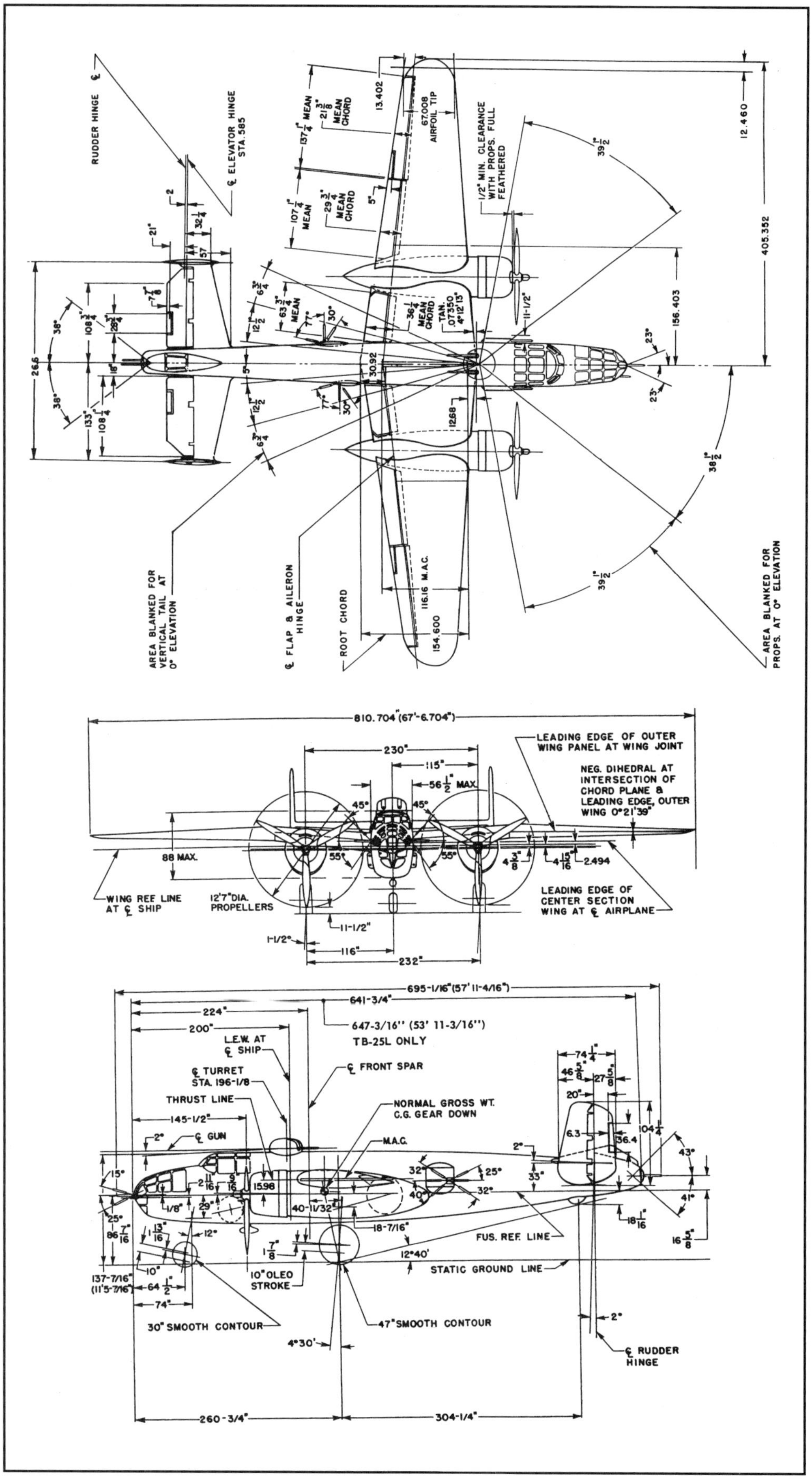

B-25J used tailguns and nose armament to advantage. (Carl Scholl)

can raid on Hanoi was a single-ship B-25 mission on 3 September, dropping bombs and pamphlets, and claiming damage to parked aircraft, munitions, and supplies.[5]

Fifth Air Force B-25s were repeatedly tasked to interdict Japanese-held roads and bridges around Port Moresby, Wairopi in the Owen Stanley range, and the Buna-Kokoda trail. The Allied air offensive preparatory to the British Eighth Army's ground attack west of El Alamein included a B-25 mission against an Axis airfield on 19 October. By 24 October, these USAMEAF (United States Army, Middle East Air Forces) B-25s were in support of the British ground troops west of El Alamein, between the Mediterranean Sea and Qattara Depression, striking troop concentrations, tent camps, vehicles and gun emplacements. On the night of 25 October, CATF sent a half dozen B-25s out on that organization's first night strike, targeting the power plant that supplied shipyards in Hong Kong, while three more B-25s bombed the mission's secondary target, a Canton warehouse area, where they caused several large fires and explosions. Through the end of this month, USAMEAF B-25s continued pounding Axis targets in support of General Montgomery's army in the battle near El Alamein.[6]

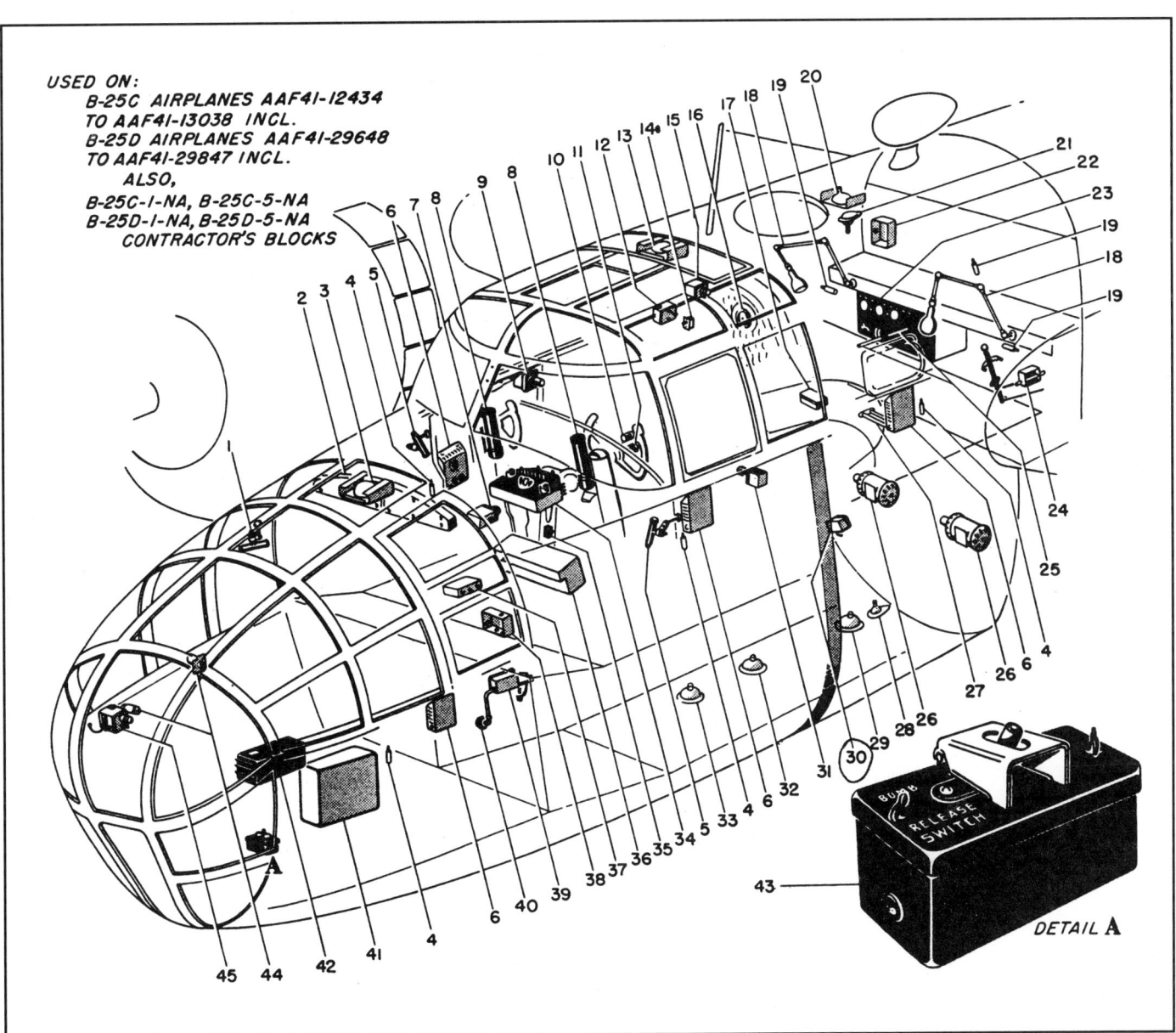

B-25C and D electrical equipment could include identification, friend or foe (IFF) lights in the bottom of the forward fuselage (part numbers 29, 32, and 33). Electric heater rheostat panels served the bombardier, pilot, copilot, and navigator in the forward fuselage (part number 6, repeated in drawing). Type A-8 fluorescent lights mounted to the pilot's and copilot's control columns, as depicted in a B-25 Dash-4 illustrated parts book. (Carl Scholl)

During the first week of November 1942, USAMEAF Mitchells targeted Axis tanks and other battlefield transport; Pacific B-25s of Fifth Air Force went after ship and shore targets. On 9 November, Fifth AF Mitchells scored a hit on a merchant ship off the southern tip of New Ireland, and attacked a schooner near Salamaua.

In November and into December 1942, Fifth AF B-25s bombed targets around hotly-contested Buna, a village tenaciously held by the Japanese. As USAAF organizational structure matured in the middle east, 12th Air Force began orchestrating some B-25 missions, as on 5 December when Mitchells hit the enemy airfield at Sidi Ahmed.

Meanwhile, Ninth Air Force B-25s nipped at retreating Axis forces in north Africa on 15 December. Two days later, a pair of B-25s added to the mix of 11th Air Force warplanes launched against north Pacific Japanese targets, although only Liberators reached their targets that day in this inclement environment.[7]

Classic photo of a dilemma for twin-engine aircraft pilots shows a 12th Bomb Group Mitchell with the right engine shut down, and the aircraft slowly descending to the Mediterranean Sea. Even after pitching overboard loose equipment, this B-25 ultimately was forced to ditch. When the photo was taken, it appears the flexible nose machine gun had already been jettisoned. (12th Bomb Group Association)

1943

Three 11th Air Force B-25s sank a 6,500-ton cargo ship off Holtz Bay in the Aleutians on 5 January 1943, advancing the reputation of the Mitchell as a ship killer. As the month played out, Aleutian B-25s several times were forced to abort missions due to inclement weather; Mediterranean Mitchells attacked transportation, airfield, and shipping targets. In the Pacific, Fifth AF B-25s continued to strike targets around Lae. On 25 January, 10th Air Force spread B-25s out on a five-ship attack that damaged a bridge at Myitnge, discouraging Japanese rebuilding efforts there; a three-ship raid on marshaling yards at Mandalay that damaged tracks,

Bomb shackles in paired mounts under the wings of B-25s increased mission flexibility by allowing more bombs to be carried, or by permitting fuel cells in the bomb bay. (NAA photo via Gene Boswell)

B-25 bombardier at work was captured in this elegantly detailed line drawing from a Mitchell manual. Three ammunition boxes in a tray to the right of the bombardier fed the flexible nose gun, which was held out of the bombardier's way by bungee cords. (Carl Scholl/Aero Trader)

cars, and the freight house; and another three-B-25 effort on marshaling yards at Naba. Two days later, off the coast of Algeria, 12th Air Force B-25s attacked two destroyers, setting fire to one of them.[8]

The first week of February 1943 saw a trio of 11th Air Force B-25s attack Kiska's Main Camp area; that week, 12th Air Force Mitchells attacked an airfield at Sfax; Fifth AF B-25s again targeted Lae, going after a Japanese airfield there; and 10th Air Force B-25s revisited a bridge at Myitnge. B-25 over the Aleutians claimed a Japanese floatplane shot down on 13 February. Northwest African Air Forces (NAAF) B-25s attacked a bridge near Kasserine Pass on 22 February as German troops began to withdraw toward Kasserine; these Mitchells continued their involvement around Kasserine and other Axis hot spots for the remainder of the month.

The month of March 1943 saw B-25s deployed around the world, with NAAF and Ninth Air

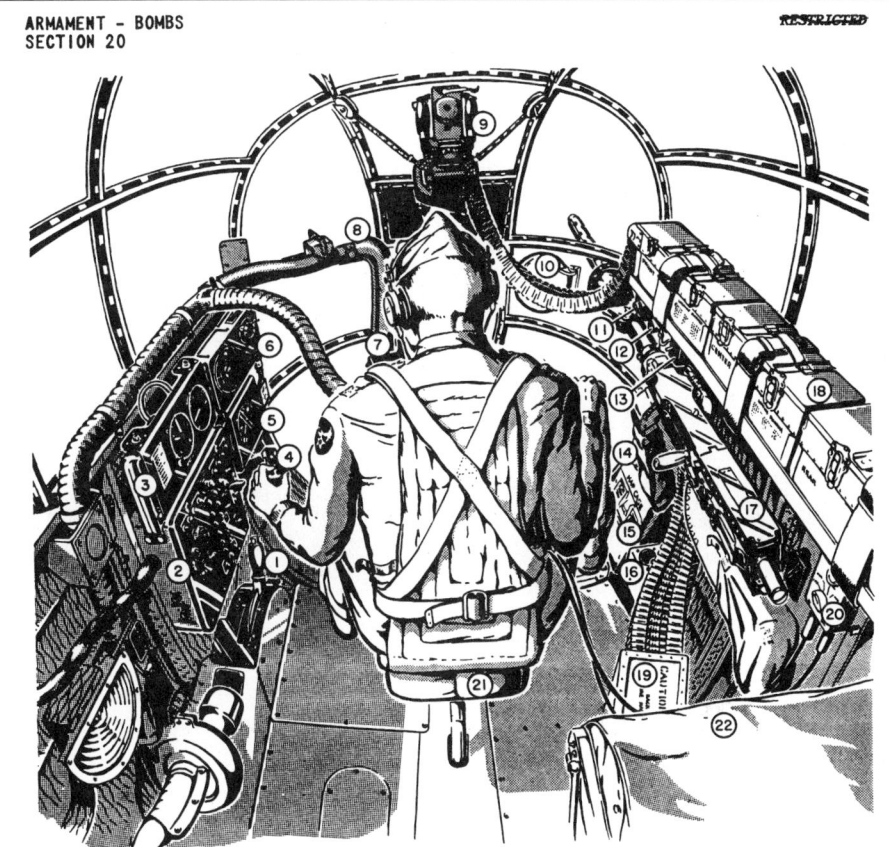

1. BOMB CONTROL HANDLE
2. BOMB CONTROL PANEL
3. INSTRUMENT PANEL
4. BOMB RELEASE SWITCH
5. COMPASS
6. BOMB INTERVAL CONTROL
7. BOMBSIGHT
8. BOMBSIGHT WINDOW HOT-AIR DUCT
9. FLEXIBLE .50-CALIBER NOSE GUN
10. BOMBSIGHT WINDOW ACCESS DOOR
11. EXTENSION LIGHT
12. ULTRA VIOLET LAMP
13. GLIDE BOMBING ATTACHMENT SELECTOR VALVE
14. MAP CASE
15. GLIDE AND CLIMB CHART
16. OXYGEN REGULATOR
17. FIXED .50 CALIBER NOSE GUN
18. FLEXIBLE GUN AMMUNITION BOXES
19. FIXED GUN AMMUNITION BOX
20. INTERPHONE CONTROLS
21. BOMBING SEAT
22. BOMBARDIER'S RIDING SEAT

Figure 463—Bomb Controls - Bombardier's Compartment

Two early B-25Cs hold formation; nearest aircraft has Bendix lower turret extended. This turret sometimes got stuck in the down position, to the detriment of the bomber's range. Lower turrets subsequently were deleted from production Mitchells, and removed from many already in service. (SDAM)

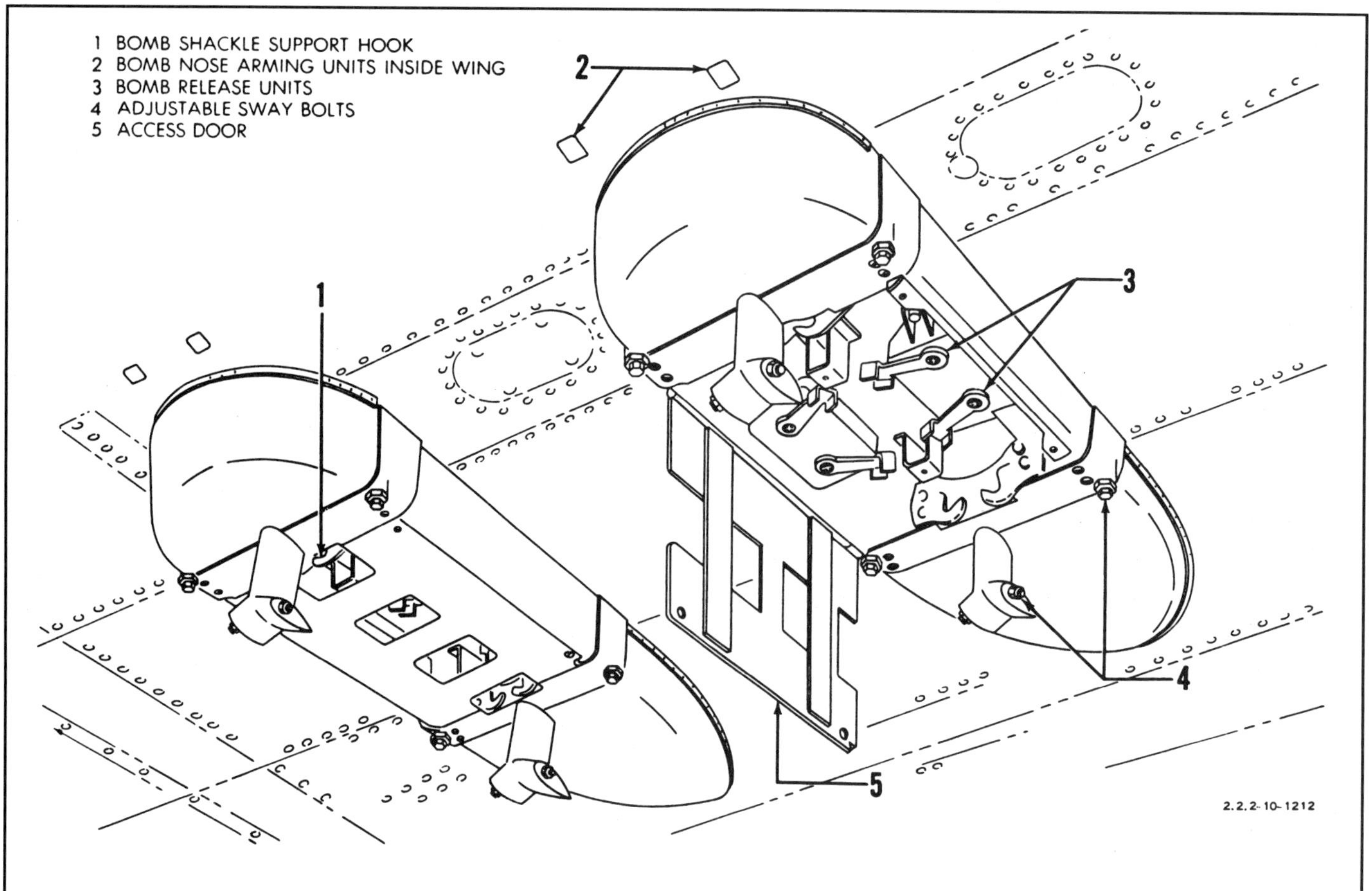

```
1  BOMB SHACKLE SUPPORT HOOK
2  BOMB NOSE ARMING UNITS INSIDE WING
3  BOMB RELEASE UNITS
4  ADJUSTABLE SWAY BOLTS
5  ACCESS DOOR
```

Figure 11-5. Wing Bomb Racks Installed

Line art from the B-25J erection and maintenance manual shows components of dual mount underwing bomb shackles. (Don Keller/Bob, Dave, and Jeff Sturges)

Force Mitchells prosecuting the war in the middle east as Fifth AF B-25s went after Japanese shipping and ports in the south Pacific; 10th Air Force B-25s circulated in the China-Burma-India (CBI) Theater as their 11th Air Force counterparts silenced Japanese anti-aircraft positions at Kiska in the misty Aleutians. In a classic example of close-air support, on 24 March 1943, Northwest African Tactical Air Force (NATAF) B-25s and A-20s hit Axis troops concentrated near El Guettar, where the U.S. Army's First Division was under attack.[9]

Kiska continued to receive attention from 11th AF B-25 crews in April 1943, while other Mitchell units around the globe continued bombing transportation and troop targets. It was a litany that was repeated, with inexorable movement toward an ultimate Allied victory still two years distant.

The second day of May 1943 saw Fifth Air Force B-25s unsuccessfully attack a ship near Toeal. Fifth Air Force improvisers including the legendary Pappy Gunn were already at work to make the Mitchell the premier commerce killer by introducing various arrays of forward-firing fuselage mounted guns, some of which led to similar installations at the NAA factory. Haiphong harbor docks reverberated under an attack by nine Mitchells from 14th Air Force on 4 May, followed by 19 P-40 escort fighters strafing the target after the B-25s bombed it. In the Mediterranean, in May 1943 Mitchells of NAAF and Ninth Air Force units repeatedly targeted enemy transportation and shipping in a war of interdiction. A dozen 11th AF B-25s was tasked to support U.S. ground troops landing on Attu on 11 May. A combined force totaling more than 80 B-25s and B-26s from NAAF units bombed targets on Pantelleria Island in conjunction with a naval blockade on 18 May and on several subsequent days that month, with the Mediterranean Mitchells and Marauders also spreading the war to Sardinia. On

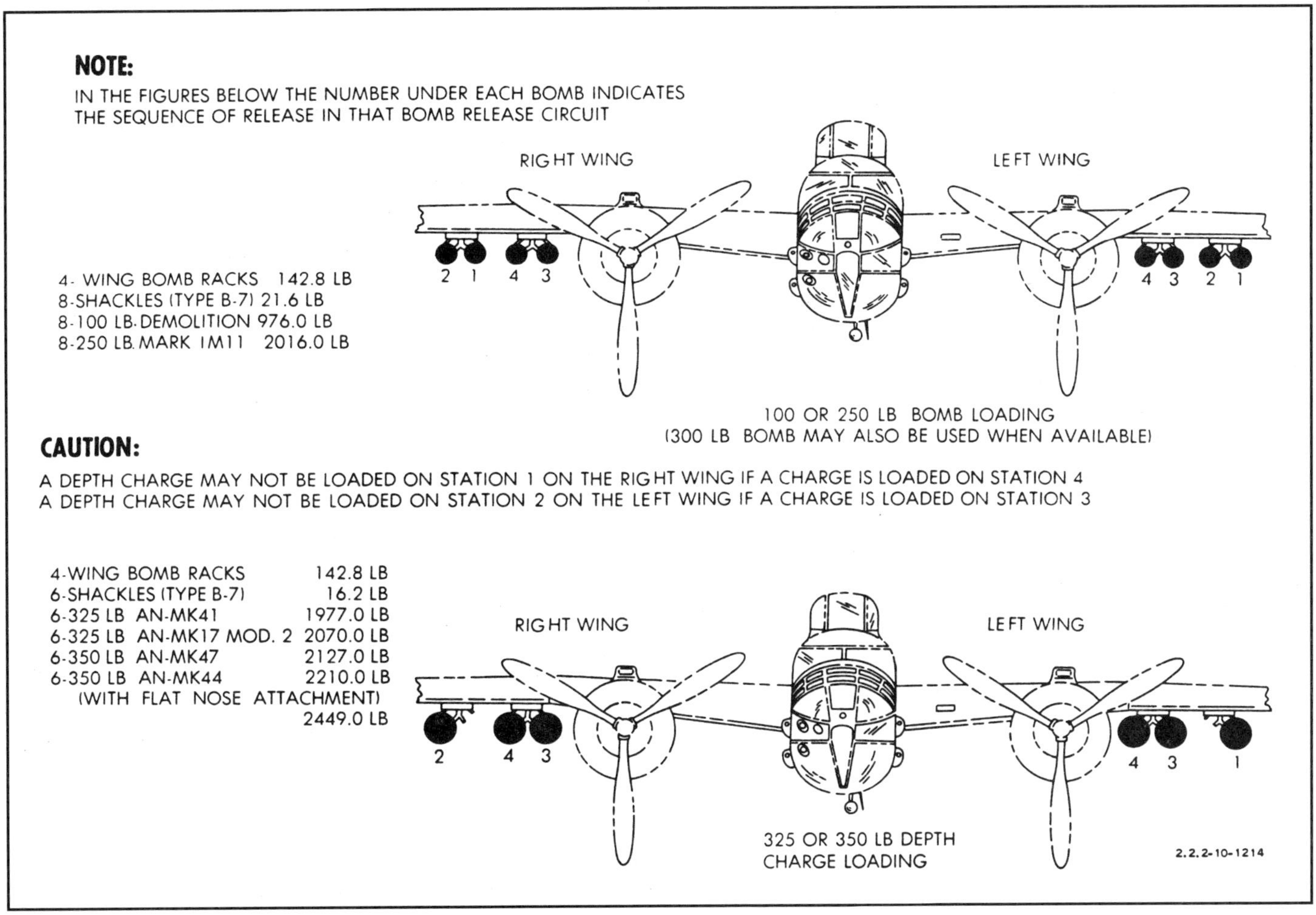

NOTE:
IN THE FIGURES BELOW THE NUMBER UNDER EACH BOMB INDICATES
THE SEQUENCE OF RELEASE IN THAT BOMB RELEASE CIRCUIT
RIGHT WING
LEFT WING
2 1 4 3
4 3 2 1
4- WING BOMB RACKS 142.8 LB
8-SHACKLES (TYPE B-7) 21.6 LB
8-100 LB-DEMOLITION 976.0 LB
8-250 LB MARK IM11 2016.0 LB
100 OR 250 LB BOMB LOADING
(300 LB BOMB MAY ALSO BE USED WHEN AVAILABLE)
CAUTION:
A DEPTH CHARGE MAY NOT BE LOADED ON STATION 1 ON THE RIGHT WING IF A CHARGE IS LOADED ON STATION 4
A DEPTH CHARGE MAY NOT BE LOADED ON STATION 2 ON THE LEFT WING IF A CHARGE IS LOADED ON STATION 3
4-WING BOMB RACKS 142.8 LB
6-SHACKLES (TYPE B-7) 16.2 LB
6-325 LB AN-MK41 1977.0 LB
6-325 LB AN-MK17 MOD. 2 2070.0 LB
6-350 LB AN-MK47 2127.0 LB
6-350 LB AN-MK44 2210.0 LB
(WITH FLAT NOSE ATTACHMENT)
2449.0 LB
RIGHT WING
LEFT WING
2 4 3
4 3 1
325 OR 350 LB DEPTH
CHARGE LOADING
2.2.2-10-1214

Depicting a glass-nosed B-25J with underwing bomb racks, this artwork from the erection and maintenance manual shows the racks' capacities. (Keller/Sturges)

27 May one 11th AF B-25 bombed and strafed Japanese troops on Attu, and dropped photographs taken the previous day to friendly forces.[10]

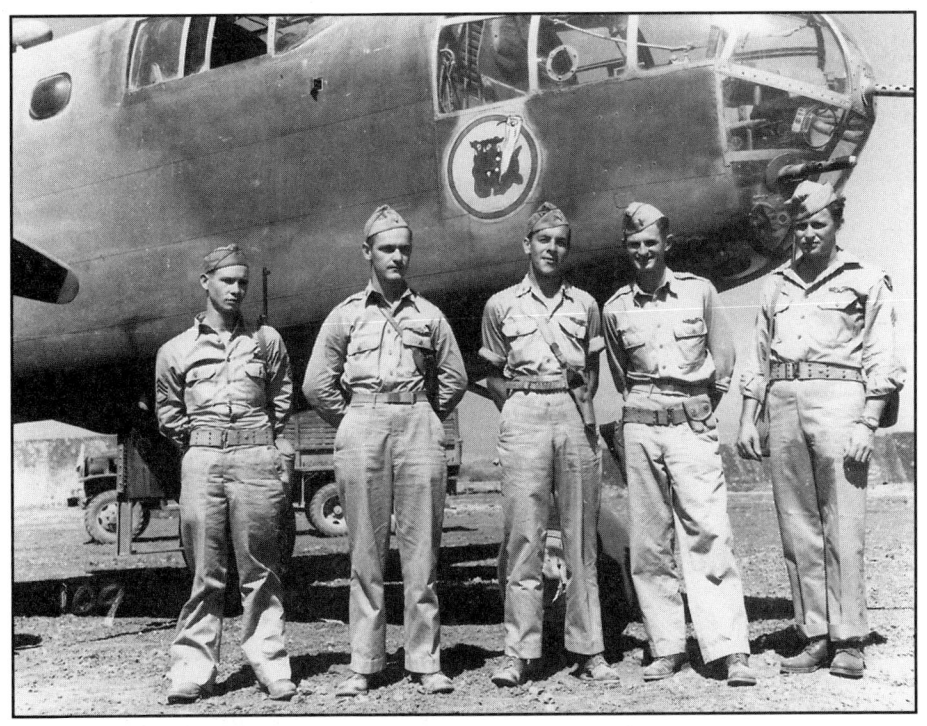

Crew of a 12th Bomb Group B-25C or D-model posed by the nose of their Mitchell in the Mediterranean Theater of Operations (MTO). On some Mitchells like this example, the fixed nose gun protruded through a metal wind baffle sleeve instead of the waterproof canvas boot depicted in tech manual artwork. This B-25 was oversprayed in irregular sections to produce a variegated camouflage, a common practice in the MTO. (12th Bomb Group Association)

U.S. Marine PBJs (B-25D equivalents) of squadron VMB-443 held formation near Emirau in the Pacific, sometime in or after August 1944. Visible on aircraft nearest camera is modified raised tail emplacement with machine gun armament. Single blister package carrying two machine guns is evident; nose has been modified to carry four fixed machine guns in addition to flexible .50-caliber weapon. (USMC photo by L.V. Smith via Bibee collection)

The air offensive against Pantelleria continued to use the services of B-25s in June 1943; the island surrendered on 11 June when the British First Division landed there unopposed. The small, yet rugged, 13th Air Force began using B-25s in the south Pacific in the spring of 1943; on 14 June of that year, 18 Mitchells from 13th AF, escorted by F4U Corsairs, attacked Vila airfield. Probing through cloud cover, on 28 June a half-dozen 11th Air Force B-25s bombed Little Kiska, Gertrude Cove, and the southern portion of the Main Camp area through holes in the undercast; some ineffective bombing on these missions resulted from faulty bomb release hardware.

In late June and into July, Pacific B-25s supported Allied ground troops including Australians at Bobdubi Ridge and U.S. Army and Marine forces invading New Georgia. Tenth Air Force B-25s returning to hit the Myitnge bridge on 3 July dropped the southernmost span into the river below. On 10 July 1943, B-25s made 11th Air Force's first attack on the Japanese home islands when eight Mitchells bombed targets on Paramushiru and environs. On 24 July, Mitchells of NAAF joined with B-17s in attacking railyards at Bologna, Italy. Fifth Air Force Mitchells finished out July 1943 by attacking barges at Hanisch Harbor and Mange, as well as targeting the Finschafen vicinity.[11]

On 6 August, Ninth AF noted more than 80 B-25 sorties against towns and roads including sites in the Adrano area. That same day, 13th AF put up 24 B-25 sorties striking supply and bivouac areas at Rekata Bay and environs. The pace of the Mitchell's war continued to mount,

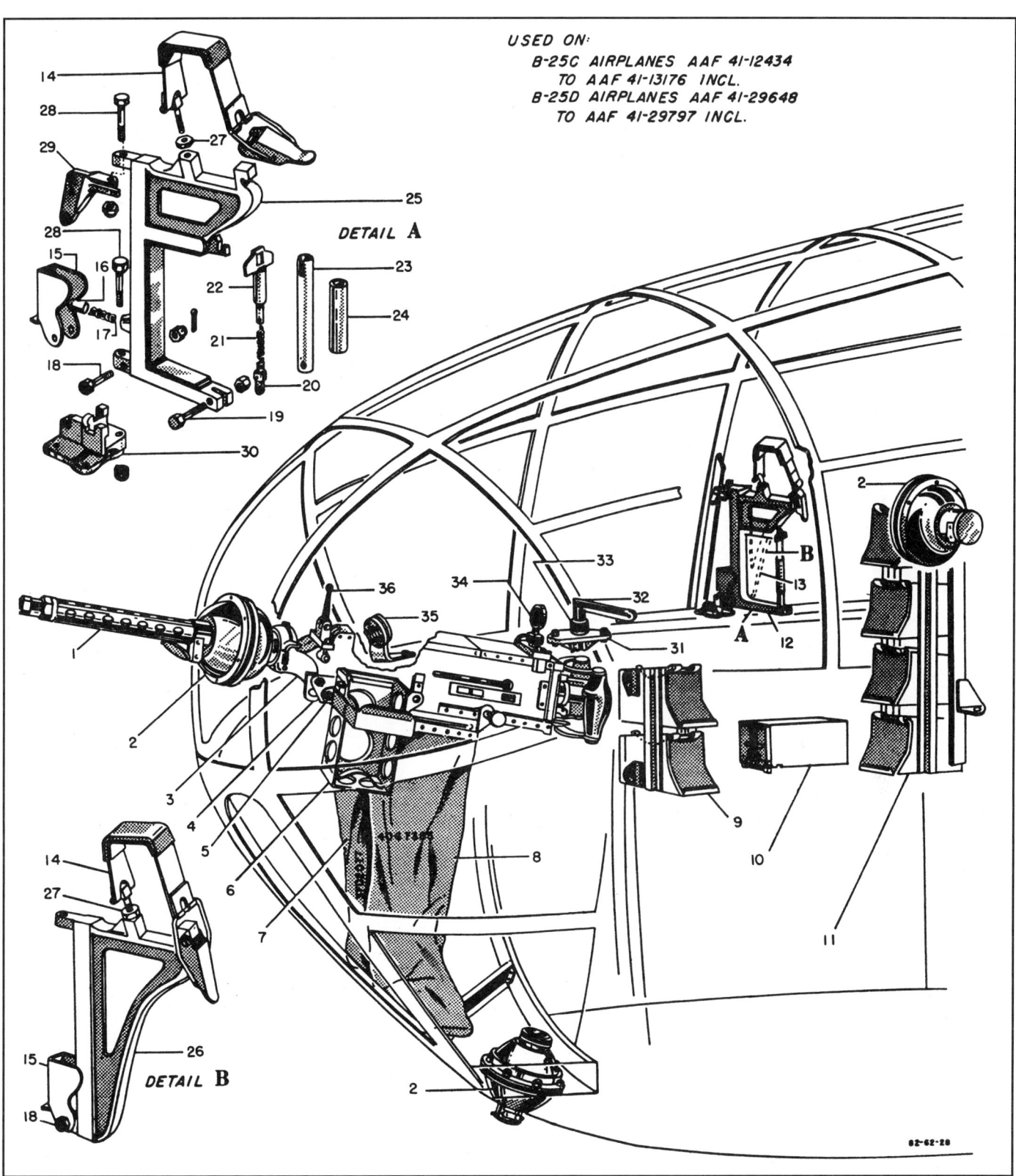

As sported by some early B-25Cs and Ds, this drawing represents a .30-caliber machine gun in a flexible socket that did not rely on a recoil adapter. This set-up used ammunition boxes to feed the gun directly, instead of running flexible chuting from a larger box. Gun could be removed from forward position and placed in socket in left side of nose. Larger .50-caliber machine gun in a recoil adapter was substituted during production run of C- and D-models. (Carl Scholl/Aero Trader)

NORTH AMERICAN B-25 MITCHELL

B-25Cs of the 12th Bomb Group formed up with RAF Martin export twin engine bombers and a P-40 escort to attack a North African target. Mitchell number 33 appears to have substituted hand-held machine guns for the lower Bendix turret. Single tail gun protrudes from Plexiglas end cap; some modifications of this type were made in the field to be triggered by the pilot in the event of an attack from the rear. (12th Bomb Group Association)

as on 7 August 1943, when 150 B-25 sorties against Randazzo were logged by Ninth Air Force. Over much of August, B-25s in the MTO bombed bridges, highways, and other transportation targets; in the south Pacific, barges were hit as the successors to Pappy Gunn's original "commerce destroyer" Mitchell conversion used forward-firing .50-calibers with good effect.[12]

For its heaviest daily total bomb tonnage to date, on 1 September 1943, Fifth Air Force put up more than 70 B-25s and four-engine B-24s to rain 201 tons of bombs on the Alexishafen-Madang area, even as other Fifth AF Mitchells attacked the Iboki Plantation, barges, and villages in New Britain, and a third contingent of B-25s from Fifth Air Force units, along with B-24s, hit targets in the Lesser Sunda Island area. The first week of September saw combat by B-25s assigned to units in Fifth, 10th, 12th, 13th, and 14th Air Forces around the world. On 11 September, a dozen B-25s from 11th Air Force, as well as eight B-24s, attacked Paramushiru for the third and final time in 1943. The Mitchell's war of interdiction saw repeated attacks by 12th Air Force B-25s on road and rail targets in Italy during this period, while in the Pacific, Fifth AF B-25s rampaged among Japanese barges in Hansa Bay and near Cape Gloucester. Fourteenth AF B-25s, often accompanied by P-40s, paid several calls on the Wuchang cotton mill this month. On 18 September 1943, 12th AF B-25Gs used their massive 75-mm cannon against small vessels and a lighthouse in the vicinity of Capraia, as well as between Pianosa and Corsica. On 22 September, Fifth Air Force B-25s attacked Japanese defenses in support of Australian *(text continued on page 69)*

A Little Color, Please

B-25 Paint and Markings

The first B-25s to enter service wore olive drab and gray camouflage. Variations appeared as early as 1942 when USAAF Mitchells sent to north Africa were painted the characteristic pinkish desert sand hue of that vicinity. Variations of sand and dark green or olive supplanted this in the Mediterranean.

Some Marine PBJ versions flew with triple-tone blue/white overwater camouflage. Some of the B-25Js supplied to the Soviet Union carried gloss black undersurfaces. Ultimately, B-25H and J-models began leaving the assembly line in natural metal finish.

Paint specifications for natural

With colored cowlings indicating different squadrons, B-25s of the 12th Bomb Group paraded over a cluttered ramp at Esler Field, Louisiana, in the first half of 1942, before the unit went to north Africa and flew Mitchells painted desert pink. The 12th Bomb Group, a scion of the pioneer Mitchell unit, the 17th Bomb Group, was activated at McChord Field near Tacoma, Washington, about a year before group member Alex Adair took this Kodachrome. (Alex Adair/12th Bomb Group Association)

In 1942, a 12th Bomb Group B-25C in olive and gray camouflage flew over Louisiana before the bomb group moved to north Africa. Large red propeller warning stripe on fuselage of early Mitchells was later deleted in wartime. (Alex Adair/12th Bomb Group Association)

NORTH AMERICAN B-25 MITCHELL

metal finish (NMF) B-25Js included the use of dull dark green inside the cockpit for anti-glare purposes. The wartime specification called for AN-TT-L-51 lacquer or AN-E-3 enamel to be used for this purpose. All compartments aft of the bomb bay (and the bombardier's compartment in the nose) were to be finished yellow-green, using AN-TT-P-656 primer tinted yellow-green. Exterior anti-glare panels were to be painted with one coat of Spec. 14109 dark olive drab camouflage enamel. B-25J requirements called for external anti-glare paint on top of the fuselage in all areas within the forward vision of the pilots, and

B-25H of the 12th Bomb Group, after the unit's 1944 move to the CBI Theater, displayed haunting fright mask used on a number of the group's Mitchells at that time. (Alex Adair/12th Bomb Group Association)

In July 1994, on the ramp at Chino, California, a haven for warbirds in the United States, one of the last Canadian fire bomber B-25Js to retire began the careful refurbishing process at Aero Trader's renowned B-25 facilities. Still under restoration in 1997, this Mitchell was slated to appear in 345th Bomb Group (Air Apaches) colors, representing a gun-nose B-25 nicknamed Betty's Dream. (Frederick A. Johnsen)

Oh Dee Whizz!, a veteran B-25J from the 12th Bomb Group, had a skin patch to protect the structure from muzzle blast of the lower blister gun; armor plating protected the fuselage from the ravages of the upper blister gun. (Bob Wilson/12th Bomb Group Association)

within lateral vision areas of the inboard sides of the engine nacelles ahead of the wing leading edge.[1]

The Hamilton-Standard aluminum propeller blades and hubs of the B-25J were to be painted flat black with the outer four inches of the tips painted "identification yellow". Visible areas of instrument panels were to be painted flat black; indirect lighting areas were to be gloss white.[2]

[1] Repair Manual — B-25J, North American Aviation report No. NA-5859. [2] *Ibid*.

Smudges from repeated firing of package guns blackened the adjacent fuselage of Blonde Betty *of the 12th Bomb Group in India circa 1945. Thick armor plating behind nose art cast a shadow where it ended; escape hatch handle was painted bright red for quick visibility in emergencies. Drift sight protruded from fuselage above B in nickname. (Alex Adair/12th Bomb Group Association)*

Snafu of the 12th Bomb Group released a British bomb over a target in north Africa in the latter part of 1942 or early 1943. RAF-style fin flash obscures part of the serial number and individual aircraft number 14 on Snafu; some other renditions retained the numerals. (Alex Adair/12th Bomb Group Association)

Jivin' Julie danced her way through combat with the 12th Bomb Group when photographed in India circa 1945. By that time, the veteran 12th Group flew a variety of bombardier-nose and solid-nose Mitchells. (Alex Adair/12th Bomb Group Association)

B-25D (43-3318) ended its military service with the Royal Canadian Air Force in the early 1960s. Photographed while still carrying its RCAF red lightning stripe, and registered N88972, the Mitchell paused in Seattle, Washington, for maintenance in March 1967 before flying to Alaska for service as a fire bomber. Subsequently flown by Merrill Wien, this D-model was sold to the Fighter Collection in Duxford, United Kingdom, in 1987. (Frederick A. Johnsen)

B-25J N10564 was used by the U.S. Forest Service in early 1961 to test suitability of the B-25 as a fire bomber after several crashes of air tanker Mitchells in California the previous fire season. Data boom extending from nose allowed U.S. Army flight testers operating at Edwards Air Force Base to obtain information. Release of fire retardant could prompt abrupt pitch-up as low pressure was created beneath aft fuselage of B-25. Ultimately banned from use by the U.S. Forest Service, B-25 fire bombers nonetheless continued to serve reliably on Canadian fires and in Alaska under contract to the Bureau of Land Management; the last Canadian Mitchell air tankers retired in the early 1990s. (AFFTC History Office collection)

How 'Boot That!?, a B-25J of the 310th Bomb Group, flew 81 combat missions in the Mediterranean Theater between September 1944 and April 1945. When Carl Scholl's Aero Trader company restored this combat Mitchell, the original artist, Ray Kowalic, was located to recreate the nose art once again. Scholl's restoration was meticulous to the point of replacing battle damage patches on new skin where portions of the veteran bomber required reskinning, to preserve its combat look. The restored B-25, owned by the Cavanaugh Flight Museum of Addison, Texas, was named Grand Champion World War Two aircraft at the Experimental Aircraft Association (EAA) Oshkosh convention in 1995, where the photo was taken. (Frederick A. Johnsen)

At Marfa Army Airfield in Texas during World War Two, a venerable B-25A (40-2204) and a B-25H (43-4633) were available for instructor proficiency flying or "diversionary training" at this Cessna AT-17 base. (USAAF/SDAM)

(text continued from page 64) ground troops that landed north of Finschhafen.[13] This period saw Pacific B-25s frequently employed in strafing attacks against barges and villages in areas where low altitude attacks were feasible; Mitchells in the Mediterranean often were used at medium altitudes in more traditional bombing formations. The concept of gunship strafer Mitchells was prevalent in the Pacific; many Mediterranean B-25Js did not even carry package guns on the forward fuselage as did most of their Pacific counterparts, indicative of the relative emphasis placed on strafing in each geographic area.[14]

Foul weather thwarted a force of 80 heavy bombers and fighters sent by Fifth Air Force against Rabaul on 18 October, but more than 50 B-25s dipped beneath the low-lying clouds to attack the town, shipping, and airfields from treetop altitude. The Mitchell crews that day

Strafer Mitchell of the 341st Bomb Group appears to have its six field-modified nose guns splayed downward at different angles to spread the pattern on the ground. Flexible ammo feed chute can be discerned for top gun in right of photo; middle gun at right uses older small clip-on ammo can.

NORTH AMERICAN B-25 MITCHELL

A PBJ-1H performed aircraft carrier trial landings and takeoffs aboard the USS Shangri-La *in November 1944. A special tailhook (not visible in this photo) was fitted to the aft fuselage.* (Peter M. Bowers collection)

claimed more than 70 aircraft destroyed on the ground and in the air, as well as two vessels sunk. On 24 October, 13th AF sent 36 Mitchells, with 24 Royal New Zealand Air Force P-40s and four Navy Corsairs, to attack Kahili airfield.[15]

The first day of November 1943 saw 15th Air Force activated at Tunis, under command of Gen. Jimmy Doolittle. That day, B-25s assigned to 15th Air Force attacked marshaling yards at Rimini and Ancona. A few days later, the two B-25 groups of 15th Air Force were transferred to 12th Air Force. On 4 November, B-25s of the Chinese-American Composite Wing of 14th Air Force flew their first combat mission, bombing and strafing troops, shipping, and supply facilities at Amoy and Swatow. These Mitchell crews claimed four cargo vessels seriously damaged, and perhaps sunk. Twelfth Air Force B-25s ranged into Albania on 5 November 1943 to attack Berat-Kucove airfield.[16]

In the south Pacific, Fifth AF B-25s sometimes operated in concert with warplanes of the Royal New Zealand and Royal Australian Air Forces, as on 13 November when USAAF Mitchells and RAAF Beaufighters claimed the sinking of a small freighter near Tanimbar Island. On 15 November, an aerial melee developed when 88 Fifth AF B-25s escorted by 16 P-40s encountered Japanese fighters that were escorting bombers of their own. The warplanes tangled, and the B-25s abandoned their bombing mission. Claims of 20 Japanese aircraft shot down were made by U.S. fliers as a result of that confrontation. On 28 November, B-25s from 12th Air Force bombed docks, warehouses, marshaling yards, shipping, and barracks, among other targets, at Zara, Sibenik, and Dubrovnik. Next day, Mitchells from 12th AF attacked Sarajevo.[17]

When Japanese troops took control

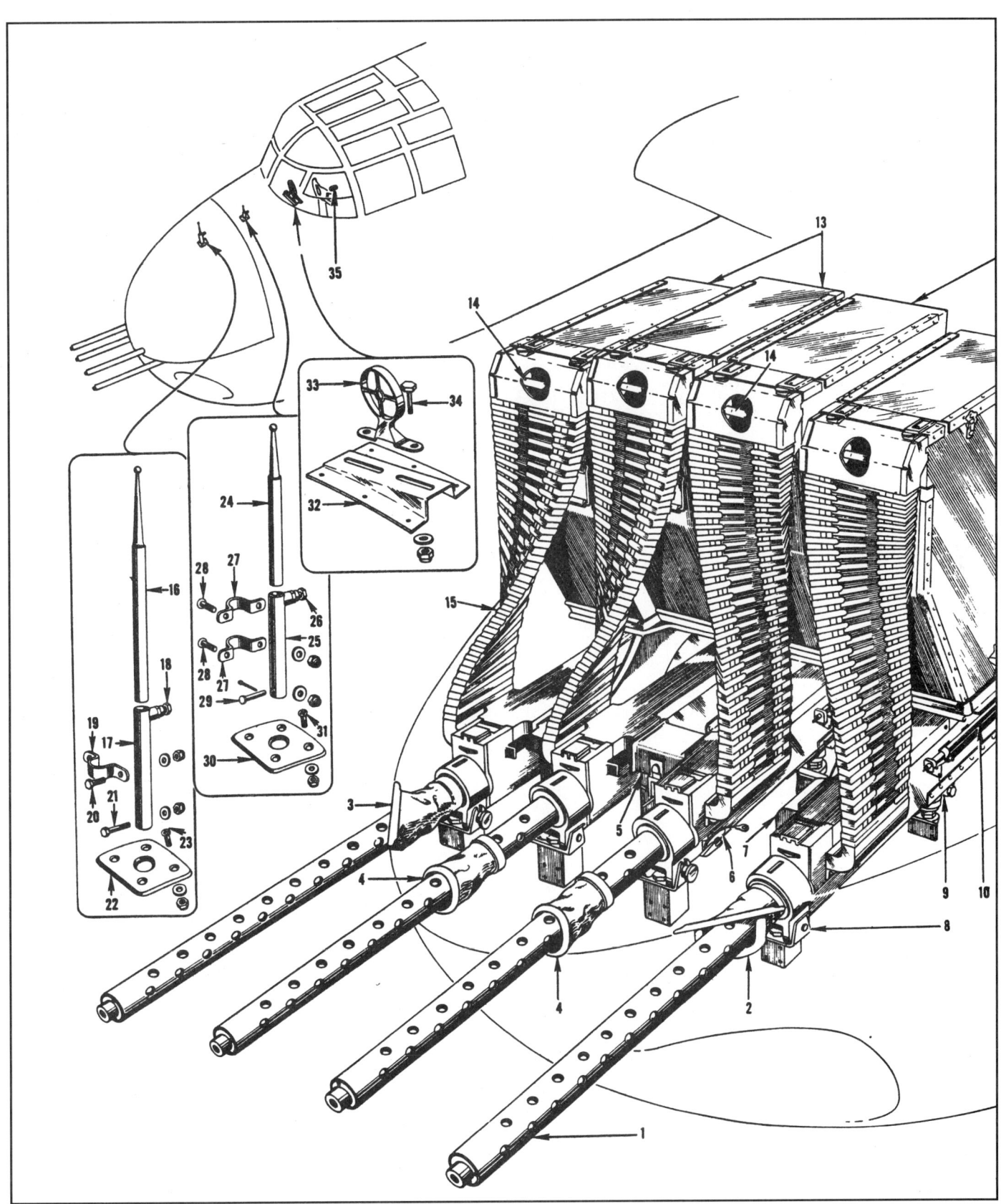

Four-gun array of M-2 .50-caliber machine guns in the nose of the B-25H used large ammunition cans connected by stainless steel flexible ammo chutes, as drawn for a Dash-4 illustrated parts book. Iron ring-and-bead sight aided pilot in putting rounds on target. (Bill Miranda collection)

Mitchells in the Mediterranean often flew at higher altitudes than their Pacific counterparts. (USAAF/Clingman/SDAM)

of Changte on 4 December 1943, 11 B-25s and a dozen P-40s of 14th AF bombed there. Eleven more B-25 sorties in two attacks were logged against Changte that day. Pressure on Changte was kept up by 14th AF for several days, as on 6 December when more than 30 Mitchell sorties there were logged.

On 14 December, B-25s were part of a 228-bomber armada from Fifth AF that placed Arawe under almost continuous attack for nine hours beginning before 7 a.m. Next day, U.S. Army troops landed on the west coast of the Arawe peninsula. Cannon-armed Mitchells of Fifth AF bombed and fired on Madang on 21 December. Fifth Air Force B-25s also participated in repeated pre-invasion attacks on Cape Gloucester in December, including Christmas day activity; U.S. Marine troops landed there on 26 December. Thirteenth Air Force B-25s paid repeat visits to Kahili as December 1943 played out. Seventh AF launched B-25 attacks from Tarawa in this time period. As 1943 drew to a close, a half-dozen 14th Air Force B-25s claimed three cargo vessels and one troop carrier sunk on the Yangtze River in the vicinity of Anking and Lu-Kuan, while another pair of Mitchells from 14th AF performed a sea sweep during which they damaged a passenger vessel in the Hainan Straits on the last day of the year.[18]

1944

January 1944 continued with the worldwide pattern of B-25 interdiction and occasional battlefield strikes. The first day of the new year produced a remarkable, and somewhat unintended, bombing tactic as 10th Air Force B-25 pilot Maj. Robert Erdin released his Mitchell's bombs as he pulled up to avoid a tree while he was attacking a bridge on the Mu River. The bombs found their way to the bridge and dropped two of its spans. The 490th Bomb Squadron refined this technique into a deliberate and deadly way to demolish bridges, earning them the nickname of Burma Bridge Busters. Seventh Air Force sent nine B-25s out for a deck-level strafing and bombing attack against ships and shore targets at Maloelap on 15 January. One of the

Vertical tail stripes and insignia on the fuselage identified this as a Free French B-25. (Bowers collection)

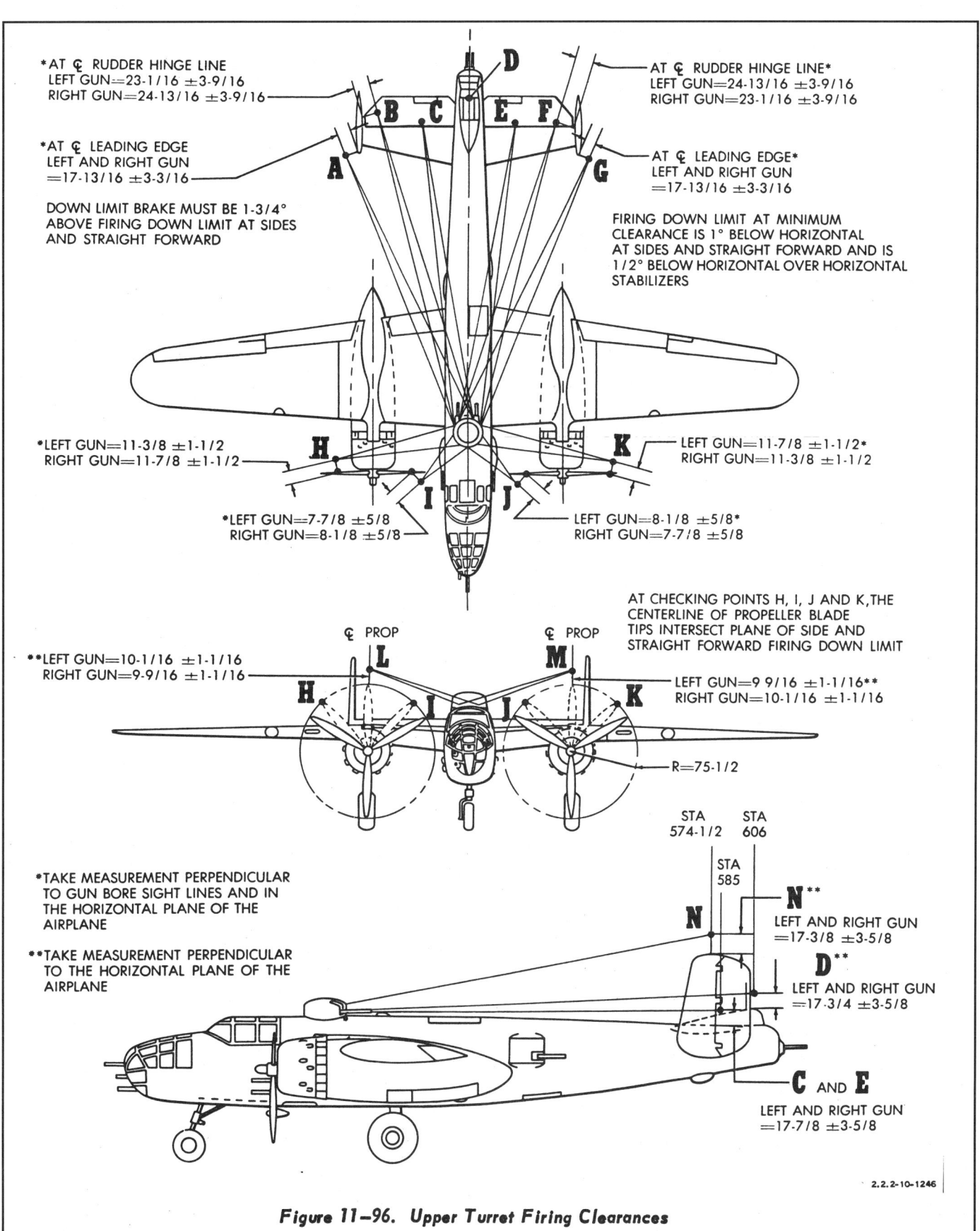

Figure 11-96. Upper Turret Firing Clearances

B-25J erection and maintenance manual drawing shows gunfire clearance limits for the top turret. (Keller/Sturges)

Nationalist Chinese B-25J featured blue insignia and rudder stripes. (Peter M. Bowers)

Mitchells crashed at sea after sustaining antiaircraft fire; the B-25s claimed damage to two vessels, hangars, an oil dump, runways, and buildings.[19]

On 18 January, 13th AF logged 34 B-25 sorties, supported by about 70 fighters, attacking Tobera. The effort to disrupt Axis transportation in Italy was exemplified by 12th Air Force B-25 attacks on various chokepoints around Rome on 21 January 1944, intended to bottle up enemy movements. On 23 January, 21 Mitchells from Seventh AF attacked Taroa Island, returning with claims of three Japanese fighters shot down. Three days later, the Mitchells of Seventh AF claimed five fighters shot down in a running battle with Japanese interceptors, joined by friendly P-40s over Aur Atoll. The P-40s claimed another 10 Japanese planes downed in that action. Visual flight conditions were important to most medium bomber operations, and on 30 January some 12th Air Force Mitchell

Snug Plexiglas tail cap on B-25 C- and D-models could accommodate an observer, or, in this case, a North American Aviation worker. A variety of field modifications restored guns, both real and mock, to this station. Some installations poked a gun muzzle through a hole cut in the clear plastic; others removed the dome altogether. (NAA/Gene Boswell)

The ultimate strafer Mitchell was the solid nose variant of the B-25J, with eight .50-caliber machine guns stacked in fours, plus four package guns. If the top turret was turned to fire forward, this Mitchell could rake a target with 14 machine guns firing simultaneously. After the war, some of the aluminum eight-gun noses, minus their armament, were used on civilian Mitchells when the glazed bombardier nose was not needed. (NAA)

The 345th Bomb Group incorporated a striking Indian head insignia on the tails of its Mitchells in the Pacific. Known as the Air Apaches, the group honored these fierce warriors whose reputation was established in the previous century in the American west. Dark circle impinging on bar of national insignia is emergency exit opening. (Ken Jordan collection)

PBJ-1H, equivalent to a B-25H, used triple-tone overwater camouflage. Faired armor-plate bullet deflectors are silhouetted immediately behind top turret gun muzzles. (SDAM)

missions over Italy had to cancel due to weather; other 12th AF B-25s got through to attack road junctions at Valmontone and Genzano di Roma, and blast the town of Monte Compatri.[20]

Fifth Air Force B-25s ranged over the coast of New Britain on 2 February 1944, between Cape Gauffre and Rein Bay, as other Fifth AF Mitchells attacked shipping near Tingwon Island and the southeast coast of New Britain. To support the U.S. Fifth Army in the face of an Axis counterattack at Anzio, 12th Air Force B-25s bombed the town of Cisterna di Latina on 7 and 8 February. Mitchells from the 12th Air Force continued in the close air support role during the Anzio contest, as on 13 February when B-25s and A-20s supported the U.S. Army north and east of the beach head by attacking vehicle and troop concentrations and an ammunition dump. To bolster forces in the CBI (China-Burma-India Theater of Operations), the veteran 12th Bomb Group took its B-25 crews from combat over Italy and departed from 12th Air Force on 14 February, moving to a new home in India.[21]

In an assault made necessary by determined German resistance, 12th Air Force B-25s and B-26s bombed the Monte Cassino Benedictine Abbey in support of Allied troops in the vicinity on 15 February 1944. Other types of 12th Air Force warplanes subsequently bombed Cassino on ensuing days as New Zealand troops secured their objective near there. Fighting around Cassino would continue for weeks.

On the leap year date of 29 February, 12th AF B-25s bombed German troops and gun emplacements west of Cisterna di Roma. Eight B-25s and seven B-24s from Fifth Air Force penetrated poor weather to attack Japanese troop positions and guns on Los Negros on the 29th of February, the day Allied amphibious forces landed on that island. Busy 13th Air Force Mitchells attacked Rabaul on the 29th, with a Navy fighter escort. And Seventh Air Force posted strikes by B-25s on Jaluit and Mille as February 1944 ended.[22]

Evenly scalloped camouflage demarcation may be a clue to Kansas City Mitchells, as seen on a D-model towed along that city's Broadway at night in April 1943 as part of a war bond display. (SDAM)

Desert sand colored B-25C (41-13167) of the 12th Bomb Group carried a metal circular patch in place of the eyeball socket originally intended for a .30-caliber machine gun in the side of the nose. Although .30-caliber socket gun mounts were unsupported in Plexiglas, the much heavier pounding administered by the forward-firing flexible .50-caliber weapon necessitated metal support structure stronger than the clear plastic. Window panel at the aft edge of the bombardier's station is an escape hatch, with a handle on the outside to aid in emergency extraction of the bombardier. Crew hatch in belly contained a telescoping ladder for entry and exit. (USAAF/NAA)

The bombardment of Los Negros Island by Fifth AF bombers including B-25s continued into early March as ground troops wrested it from Japanese control. Fourteenth Air Force activity on 4 March 1944 included two Chinese-crewed B-25s, which, with four P-38s, claimed a tanker, freighter, and a motor launch sunk in the vicinities of Wuhu and Shihhweiyao. That same day, six more 14th AF Mitchells struck at Japan's tenuous raw materials network by bombing a chromium mine at Thanh Hoa —

Leaving no bare aluminum, NAA workers autographed Bones *before it went to the 12th Bomb Group, where it was photographed in India. Waist gun uses E-11 recoil adapter with B-25-unique lugs attached to balancing cables overhead. (12th Bomb Group Association)*

(Above) The crew of Bones *gathered at planeside before another bombing mission in the CBI Theater. Even the black ADF teardrop antenna housing received autographs on this signed Mitchell. (12th Bomb Group Association)*

clearly, this was to be a long-term war, with raw materials receiving attention as worthy targets. The Allied island-hopping push throughout the Pacific allowed Seventh Air Force B-25s on 10 March to operate from Eniwetok Atoll's Engebi, only secured on 22 February by ground forces; these Mitchells attacked Kusaie Island.[23]

Young warriors in A-2 jackets pose by the nose of Bones *in India. Patch where 75MM cannon was removed was autographed as was the rest of the bomber. (12th Bomb Group Association)*

Cannon-firing Mitchells of Seventh Air Force ranged from Tarawa to bomb and strafe targets on 18 March 1944. Fifth AF B-25s joined the forces repeatedly hitting Wewak during this time period. Seventh AF Mitchells from Eniwetok attacked Ponape on 25 March, claiming four Japanese fighters shot down during the action. Thirteenth Air Force B-25s paid repeat visits to Ratawul, as they did on the last day of March 1944. Other 13th AF Mitchells occasionally flew night heckling missions over Rabaul during this time.[24]

During part of April, Seventh Air Force B-25s repeatedly staged shuttle missions, such as on the 11th of the month when Mitchells from the Gilbert Islands attacked Ponape, recovered and rearmed at Majuro, and then bombed Jaluit and Maloelap. In 10th Air Force, 11 B-25s attacked a Japanese supply and bivouac area near Manywet on 20 April. That day, 13th AF sent 22 Mitchells against the Matupi supply area. On 24 April, a flight of 14th Air Force B-25s on a sea patrol used their cannon on two small steamers near Cape Bastion, leaving one

A stick of 500-pound bombs dropped smoothly from the 12th Bomb Group's autograph-festooned Bones *in the CBI Theater on a medium-altitude mission.* (12th Bomb Group Association)

ship burning and claiming the other vessel sunk. Shifting from interdiction to army support as needed, Fifth AF B-25s bombed Japanese troop areas in the vicinity of Hollandia on 25 April 1944.[25]

The third day of May 1944 saw 12th Air Force B-25s attack railroad bridges in Italy as part of the ongo-

Rudimentary fire bombing in the CBI included the use of 55-gallon gas drums with bomb stabilizing fins attached. (12th Bomb Group Association)

When the B-25B entered British service it was designated Mitchell Mk 1. Photo shows first one (number FK-161) in RAF camouflage. (Peter M. Bowers collection)

ing effort to interdict German supplies and bottle them up as far from the front as possible. Two days later, 10th AF Mitchells and other aircraft were arrayed against Japanese troops in support of friendly ground forces in the Mogaung Valley. The attacks by 10th AF Mitchells would continue in this region. Even

Desert pink B-25s of the 12th Bomb Group adopted North African markings dictates of the British for Allied recognition features, including, in some cases, star insignia on both wings, and red-white-and-blue fin flashes on insides and outsides of vertical fins. Presence of black de-icer boots indicates photo was taken not long after 12th Group's arrival in the mideast. (Air Force via Bowers collection)

Not often photographed in the Mediterranean Theater of Operations, a B-25G in desert tan camouflage received attention to get it out of mud. Nickname Shady Lady *beneath silhouetted female form was painted on right side of nose.* (Air Force)

Classic tri-color white and blue maritime camouflage scheme adorned this B-25J delivered for use by the U.S. Marine Corps as a PBJ. (Bowers collection)

B-25H (AAF serial 43-4482) actually became USMC PBJ-1H Bureau of Aeronautics (BuAer) number 35281. Righthand wingtip carried podded search radar. (U.S. Navy via Peter M. Bowers)

as the numbers of available B-25s increased in most theaters during this time, solo Mitchell missions from the Aleutians were still logged, as on 13 May when a lone 11th AF B-25 flew a shipping strike and strafed two fishing boats. A pair of 11th AF Mitchells connected with a Japanese auxiliary vessel near the Kurils on 18 May, sending the ship to the bottom; that night, another pair of B-25s from 11th AF sank another of the watercraft shortly before midnight. As May drew to a close, B-25s of Fifth and 10th Air Forces repeatedly were assigned to close air support missions, hitting Japanese troops on behalf of friendly forces, instead of the sometimes longer-term job of interdiction.[26]

Japanese activity in the Imphal Valley demanded attention from ground forces and 10th Air Force, so in early June 1944 Mitchells were impressed to fly ammunition in to the area. Armed bombers sometimes found favor for combat supply missions since they were better able to defend themselves and provide groundfire suppression than were unarmed transports. Mitchells from 10th AF performed this activity almost daily for the remainder of the month. Chinese troops on the Salween front received airdropped supplies from 14th AF B-25s on 6 July 1944. The bridge busting specialty was exercised by 12th Air Force B-25s over Italy on 22 July when spans at Ronco Scrivia and Cogoli were tar-

geted, following with more bridge attacks in the Po Valley the next day. And on 23 July 1944, forward-moving Pacific campaigns saw Seventh AF Mitchells begin arriving on Saipan, from where they would subsequently reach out to strike at Tinian.[27]

Support for Operation Dragoon, the invasion of southern France, prompted 12th Air Force B-25s and other bombers and fighters to attack gun positions along the French and Italian coastline west of Genoa, timed as the assault force began moving from the vicinity of Naples toward southern France on 11 August 1944. On 14 August, B-25s, B-26s, and fighters of 12th AF supported the invasion with

82

NAA worker paused with a tug pulling a shiny new B-25J intended for the Soviet Union. Shiny black undersurfaces and variegated upper surfaces were evident on this Mitchell. (NAA)

Nicknamed Bones, *the last of 1,000 B-25Hs — also the final B-25 to be built at Inglewood — was covered with painted signatures and names of NAA employees when it was built in the summer of 1944. This Mitchell, number 43-5104, reached the 12th Bomb Group in India before the end of the year. (NAA via Peter M. Bowers)*

In flight overseas, Bones, the 1000th and last B-25H built, shows the numerals 1000 painted near the leading edges of both wings. Semicircular patches on leading edges are landing light clear covers. (12th Bomb Group Association)

attacks on beaches, troop concentrations, and gun emplacements along the French coast. Later that day, these warplanes ranged farther inland in a bridge-busting interdiction campaign to keep supplies from reaching the German troops defending their hold on southern France. Japanese combat capability in India dwindled by 16 August 1944 as 10th AF Mitchells bombed Indaw. The following day, India was effectively rid of all Japanese forces, but other targets remained in southeast Asia for the Mitchells stationed there. On 19 August, B-25s and B-26s of 12th Air Force carried the war of interdiction to the bridges of southern France.[28]

September opened with B-25s from 12th Air Force making telling hits on road and rail bridges north and northeast of Venice. Also on the first of the month, a dozen B-25s from 14th Air Force dropped bombs on Kai Tek airfield as well as a supply depot south of Canton. Next day, 12th AF B-25s bombed three bridges in the Po Valley, a scenario repeated in this time period. In the Pacific, Far East Air Forces (FEAF) B-25s attacked Morotai on 2 September; it was not uncommon for Mitchells to target islands that subsequently became new bases for B-24 Liberators and other aircraft as Allied troops wrested the real estate from the Japanese. The first USAAF medium bomber raid on the Philippines since 1942 was a FEAF Mitchell strike against Buayan Airfield on 6 September. On 9 September, an 11th Air Force B-25 with one engine out made an emergency landing at Petropavlovsk in the Soviet Union following a shipping sweep off Paramushiru. Around the globe, B-25s were available to the USAAF in sufficient numbers to mount meaningful attacks in most theaters except the European Theater of Operations (ETO), where B-25s were not deployed by the Eighth or Ninth Air Forces.[29]

In October 1944, the worldwide combat schedule of USAAF B-25s continued, as with 25 Seventh Air Force Mitchells that launched from the Marshall Islands on 9 October to bomb Truk. War in the stormy north Pacific became a series of offensive raids to remote Japanese sites by 11th AF bombers including

The autographed Bones *was faded and weathered in the CBI when photographed with the Bendix top turret dome removed for maintenance.* (12th Bomb Group Association)

the quartet of B-25s that roared over Shimushiru and Paramushiru to explode three structures, and to inflict damage on two more buildings at Cape Namikawa on 11 October. The Mitchells of 11th AF occasionally drew Japanese fighters into battle, as on 18 October when four B-25s sent to bomb Kurabu Cape airfield and Suribachi were bounced by a force estimated at between eight and 12 interceptors; the B-25 crews claimed two victories. Next day, 12th AF B-25s attacked bridges in the vicinity of Milan. While inclement weather grounded 12th Air Force B-25s much of the remainder of the month, in the newly-divided China and India-Burma Theaters, 10th AF Mitchells destroyed four bridges and damaged two more on 30 October.[30]

One of 11th AF's persistent B-25s was shot down in an engagement between about 20 Japanese fighters and four Mitchells in the vicinity of Torishima Island on 6 November 1944. FEAF Mitchells attacked Pegun Island on 14 November as a prelude to Allied amphibious landings there the next morning.[31]

Though characterized as a mechanized war, World War Two held some anachronisms, like horses and mules used to transport military supplies. On 8 December, four B-25s from 14th Air Force attacked the Nan Tan area, and killed many horses. Supported by fighters, FEAF B-25s bombed Fabrica airfield on 19 December. B-25s from 10th AF accounted for about eight bridges knocked out of commission on 20 December. Fourteenth Air Force sent eight Mitchells out to strike sites on the Burma Road on 23 December, as 13 other 14th AF B-25s ranged over towns, trains and targets of opportunity at Vinh, from Dap Cau to Lungchow, and Lang Son to Yungning. On Christmas day, 1944, B-25 action included Mediterranean Allied Tactical Air Force (MATAF) Mitchells on a supply run over Yugoslavia.

1945

USAAF B-25s continued service right up to the end of the war in the Pacific; photos of the Japanese surrender delegation arriving on Ie Shima in August also depicted decorated B-25s of the Air Apaches in attendance. In January of that year, FEAF Mitchells repeatedly attacked airfields in the central Philippines;

Bones, the 1000th B-25H, later flew with an aluminum patch where the 75MM cannon once sprouted. Newer nose art and graffiti were added as the aircraft served in the 12th Bomb Group. (12th Bomb Group Association)

10th AF B-25s flew an airfield sweep over Laihka, Kunlon, Aungban, and Mong Long airdromes on 5 January; on 15 January, 18 B-25s from 14th Air Force attacked Hankow; on the 21st of the month, 12th Air Force Mitchells targeted bridges at Lavis

B-25H *Eatin' Kitty* was assigned 12th Bomb Group aircraft number 34, painted in white on its olive drab tail. Grimacing faces adorned several 12th BG Mitchells in the CBI Theater. (12th Bomb Group Association)

Silver Lady, a B-25H of the 12th Bomb Group, shows evidence of muzzle blasts from its package guns. Damage from top gun was confined to the thick cockpit armor plate, while lower gun was adjacent to an extra skin plate on the fuselage. About 300 B-25Hs were built with package guns on the right side only; later examples carried package guns on both sides. Silver Lady was serial 43-4603, and carried identifying number 31 in black on the vertical tail surfaces. (12th Bomb Group Association)

and Rovereto, and destroyed another bridge at Pontetidone, as well as blasting a railroad fill at San Michele all'Adige, and a supply cache at Cremona. With the number of B-25s on USAAF inventory declining from the high mark posted at the end of July 1944 (see Chapter 2), it is not surprising that references to Mitchell activities in combat theaters decline over time.[32]

February began with 10th Air Force Mitchells ruining the Mong Pawn bridge, while FEAF B-25s attacked Puerto Princesa. On the seventh of the month, 10th Air Force B-25s faced a relative curiosity — Japanese tanks — at Man Namman. FEAF sent groups of Mitchells against Bataan as well as bridges in southern Formosa on 15 February 1944. And FEAF B-25s closed out the month by napalming Sanga Sanga airfield.[33]

In one of the most unusual actions of the Mitchell's war, on 3 March 1945, 10 B-25s and about 80 fighter-bombers from 10th Air Force attacked Japanese troops, tanks, supplies, trucks, guns, and elephants used for transport behind enemy lines in Burma. Twelfth Air Force B-25s made a rare incursion into Austria on 11 March 1945 when Mitchells from the 57th Bomb Wing bombed a bridge at Drauburg.[34]

April 1945 opened as 10 B-25s from 10th Air Force flew behind Japanese lines in central Burma in an effort to cut off roads and bridges. Twelfth Air Force Mitchells bombed five bridges in northern Italy and Austria on the fifth day of April, in a continuing effort by MTO B-25s to interdict Axis movements. For the first time in 11th Air Force operations, B-25s dropped napalm incendiary bombs intended to wipe out Japanese radar installations at

Close-up of professional-quality nose art on a B-25J in the MTO also shows details of paint chipping, and size and placement of mission symbols. (SDAM)

Hayakegawa, Kotani Shima, and Minami Cape on 6 April. Successes by 11th AF crews were made all the more significant by the number of cancellations due to weather and other problems encountered in the hostile north Pacific.[35]

Early May 1945 saw FEAF B-25s supporting Australian troops on Tarakan Island; on the other side of the world, inclement weather grounded 12th AF Mitchells often during this time. On 3 May, MATAF B-25s dropped leaflets over German troops in parts of northern Italy in an effort to ensure the enemy units had learned of the unconditional surrender of all of their forces in Germany effective 2 May. With combat operations at an end with the total surrender of German forces effective 9 May, the European war of USAAF Mitchell bombers was over. On 10 May, 15 B-25s from 11th Air Force departed Attu and attacked shipping between Kashiwabara and Kataoka; flak downed one of these Mitchells, while another made an emergency landing in the Soviet Union. During this time, 14th AF B-25s repeatedly hit transportation targets to hinder Japanese withdrawal from areas of southern and eastern China. Busy B-25 activity on 19 May included a sweep of the western coast of Formosa by FEAF Mitchells. On 26 May, 14th AF logged a dozen B-25s used with six Mustangs in an attack that damaged two bridges north of Hankow.[36]

In June 1945, Gen. George C. Kenney, Fifth Air Force commander, made note of an inspection tour he made with Gen. Douglas MacArthur to the area around Brunei Bay, during which they watched as B-25s efficiently neutralized a Japanese gun emplacement in one pass over the target.[37] This month, Mitchells from FEAF, 11th, and 14th Air Force continued to log combat time. The sometimes-touchy relationship between 11th AF airmen and the Soviet military was starkly underlined on 9 June when eight Mitchells, beset by an equal number of Japanese fighters over Araido, raced over Kamchatka in an effort to avoid the interceptors. Soviet antiaircraft gunners downed one of the Mitchells that day, killing its crew in the process. Fourteenth Air Force B-25s and P-51s destroyed a pair of bridges near Quang Tri and My Chanh on the 20th of the month.

In July 1945, Seventh Air Force sent B-25s from Okinawa over Japanese targets, including Chiran airfield on Kyushu, several times. On 5 July, eight Mitchells from 14th AF sank several junks and sampans at Haiphong. And 11th AF B-25s flew a number of shipping sweeps.[38]

Wartime photo of How 'Boot That!? *shows nose art extending over the thick armor plate protecting the side of the cockpit. This Mitchell was restored by Carl Scholl and Tony Ritzman's Aero Trader company, and flown as an award winner at the 1995 Experimental Aircraft Association convention in Oshkosh, Wisconsin. (USAAF/SDAM)*

The first of August saw FEAF Mitchells attack docks and related targets at Nagasaki. On 6 August, the day Hiroshima was hit with an atomic bomb dropped by a B-29 Superfortress, FEAF B-25 Mitchells were part of a

A Green Dragon B-25 of the 38th Bomb Group's 405th Bomb Squadron, Fifth Air Force, with colorful art that came to typify Pacific Mitchells. Staggered placement of stacks of four machine guns on top of each other is evident. (Fred LePage)

F-10 from 91st Photo Mapping Squadron in natural metal finish shows dark anti-glare panel and striping around windows, probably in black. Cheek-mounted cameras had low oblique coverage out both sides of the F-10's path of flight. (Don Keller collection)

force attacking Kagoshima. Mitchells of 14th Air Force and FEAF were active on 9 August, when the second and final atomic bomb was dropped, on Nagasaki, by a B-29. For the next five days, FEAF B-25s rampaged among Japanese shipping off Korea, Kyushu, and the Inland Sea, ending on 14 August.

The Japanese treaty delegation flying in two specially-marked Mitsubishi Betty bombers to Ie Shima was escorted part way by a B-25 of the Air Apaches. For the United States, the Mitchell's reliable combat service was at an end, although B-25s would continue to serve the postwar USAF in training and utility roles for more than a decade.

MITCHELLS IN MISHAPS

The USAAF tracked aircraft mishap rates during World War Two. In the continental United States, where training new crews took a toll on all types of aircraft, the average mishap rate for B-25s between 1942 and August 1945 was 33 per 100,000 flying hours. This compared with a rate of 55 per 100,000 flying hours for less-forgiving Martin B-26s, 35 for B-24s, 30 for B-17s, and 40 per 100,000 flying hours for B-29s. The twin-engine Douglas A-20 posted a wartime stateside total accident rate of 131 per 100,000 flying hours.[39]

The B-25 stateside mishap rate was as high as 104 per 100,000 flying hours in 1942, as training geared up for the long war ahead. Likely attributable to increased experience with the aircraft, the stateside B-25 mishap rate dropped in 1943 to 44, and then down to 24 per 100,000 flying hours for 1944 as well as the period up to August 1945. Stateside mishap rates for the B-26 and A-20 remained higher than those of the Mitchell throughout the war, although they also showed declines, probably because experience was gained at training facilities.[40]

Between 1942 and August 1945, 446 Mitchells were listed as wrecked in accidents in the United States; B-25s not destroyed in their mishaps boosted the total stateside accidents involving Mitchells during that same time to 921 aircraft.[41]

[1] *Ibid.* [2] *Ibid.* [3] *Ibid.* [4] George C. Kenney, *General Kenney Reports*, Duell, Sloan, and Pearce, New York, 1949; reprinted by Office of Air Force History, Washington, DC, 1987. [5] Kit C. Carter and Robert Mueller, compilers, *Combat Chronology 1941-1945 — U.S. Army Air Forces in World War II*, Center for Air Force History, Washington, DC, 1991. [6] *Ibid.* [7] *Ibid.* [8] *Ibid.* [9] *Ibid.* [10] *Ibid.* [11] *Ibid.* [12] *Ibid.* [13] *Ibid.* [14] Discussion, author with B-25 restorer Tony Ritzman, 8 March 1997. [15] Kit C. Carter and Robert Mueller, compilers, *Combat Chronology 1941-1945 — U.S. Army Air Forces in World War II*, Center for Air Force History, Washington, DC, 1991. [16] *Ibid.* [17] *Ibid.* [18] *Ibid.* [19] *Ibid.* [20] *Ibid.* [21] *Ibid.* [22] *Ibid.* [23] *Ibid.* [24] *Ibid.* [25] *Ibid.* [26] *Ibid.* [27] *Ibid.* [28] *Ibid.* [29] *Ibid.* [30] *Ibid.* [31] *Ibid.* [32] *Ibid.* [33] *Ibid.* [34] *Ibid.* [35] *Ibid.* [36] *Ibid.* [37] George C. Kenney, *General Kenney Reports*, Duell, Sloan, and Pearce, New York, 1949; reprinted by Office of Air Force History, Washington, DC, 1987. [38] Kit C. Carter and Robert Mueller, compilers, *Combat Chronology 1941-1945 — U.S. Army Air Forces in World War II*, Center for Air Force History, Washington, DC, 1991. [39] *Army Air Forces Statistical Digest — World War II*, USAAF Office of Statistical Control, December 1945. [40] *Ibid.* [41] *Ibid.*

New Jobs

Post-War B-25 Operators

The B-25 was one of the lucky veterans of World War Two to survive in numbers as a result of its desirable traits. The U.S. Air Force kept predominantly converted J-models in service as late as 1959 as trainers. The following year, the last active-duty B-25 staff transport was retired by the Air Force.

More than 1,000 B-25s had received modifications or other attention at the facilities of Hayes Aircraft Corp. in Birmingham, Alabama, between August 1951 and the first quarter of 1956, when Hayes' Mitchell work was still in progress. (Multiple visits by the same B-25s for IRAN [Inspection and Repair as Necessary] and other work could account for this high tally of postwar B-25 business.) Modifications available at Hayes for postwar USAF B-25s included fire detectors, modern heating systems, new Bendix carburetors (distinguishable by higher, boxy carburetor intake scoops), new radios, and a redesigned electrical system. In serving its USAF customer, Hayes devised B-25 modification kits that could be installed in the field. In some ways, in the 1950s, Hayes Aircraft performed engineering modification tasks on the B-25 that NAA, the prime contractor, would have done a decade earlier.[1]

Hayes delivered 79 TB-25L and 380 TB-25N pilot trainers between 1952 and 1954. According to NAA B-25 engineer Norm Avery, at least some of the Hayes-modified TB-25s had exhaust semi-collector rings replacing the single stacks on the top seven cylinders of each power-

Postwar J-model Mitchell with red stripes served USAF Instrument School when photographed in April 1957. (Sumney via Peter M. Bowers collection)

Yellow and red trim adorned a B-25J used for stability-and-control instruction in the USAF test pilot school at Edwards Air Force Base, California, circa 1953. Nose art featured comic strip character Howland Owl riding an airplane. (USAF)

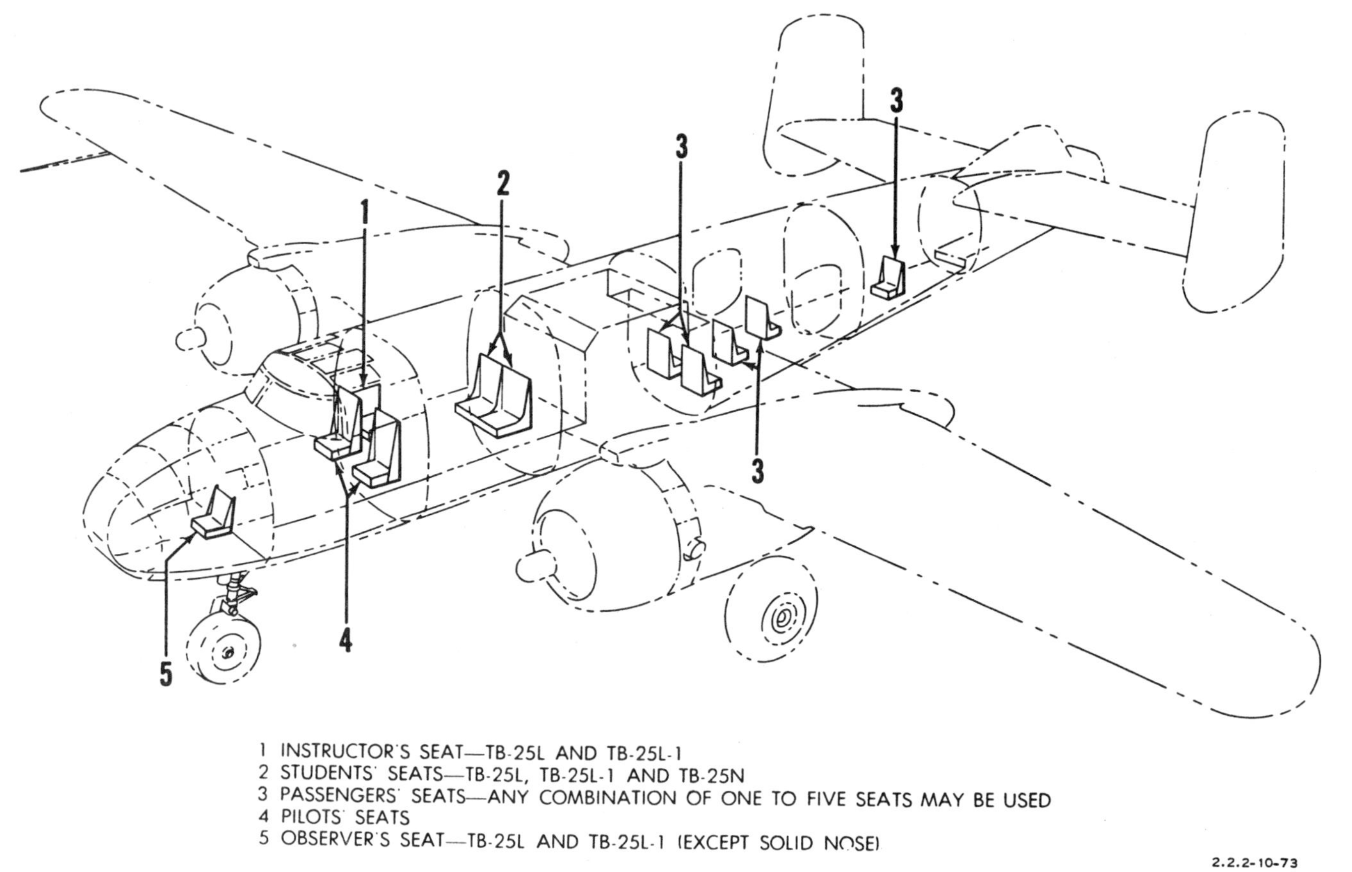

1
2
3
3
3
4
5
1 INSTRUCTOR'S SEAT—TB-25L AND TB-25L-1
2 STUDENTS' SEATS—TB-25L, TB-25L-1 AND TB-25N
3 PASSENGERS' SEATS—ANY COMBINATION OF ONE TO FIVE SEATS MAY BE USED
4 PILOTS' SEATS
5 OBSERVER'S SEAT—TB-25L AND TB-25L-1 (EXCEPT SOLID NOSE)
2.2.2-10-73

Figure 2–43. Seating Arrangement

TB-25L and N seating arrangements accommodated an instructor, students, and an observer. Drawing appeared in a B-25J manual, since postwar TB-25s were converted from J-models. (Keller/Sturges)

U.S. AIR FORCE
BD-327
0-431327

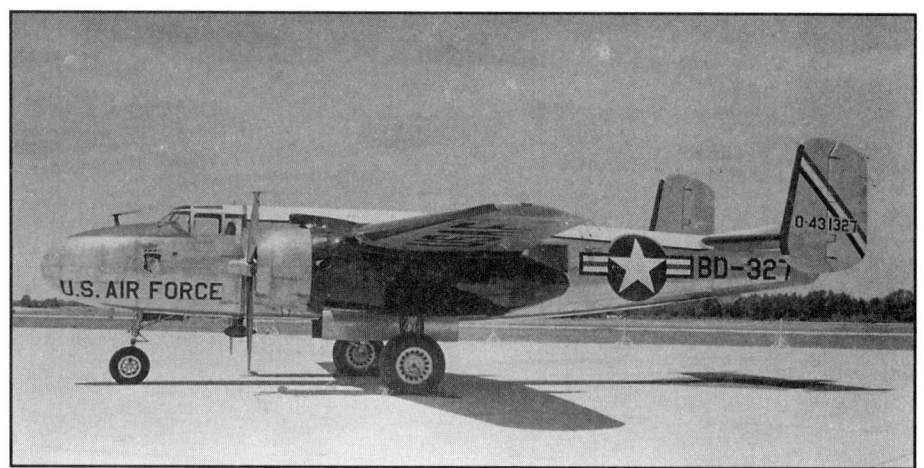

VB-25N performed transport duties with the USAF ARDC. Buzz number (BD-327) repeats last three digits of aircraft's serial number; letter B indicates bomber, and D was the letter assigned for B-25s, intended to aid in identifying specific aircraft for a variety of purposes including low-flight complaints. Many postwar B-25s received revised collector exhausts instead of individual stacks. (Shipp collection via SDAM)

plant.[2] Vibration and gravity were blamed as conspirators that could crack the upper individual stacks, making a collector ring for the top exhausts desirable.[3]

Hughes Aircraft also modified B-25Js after World War Two, producing 117 TB-25Ks and about 40 TB-25Ms as flying classrooms for Hughes' E-1 and E-5 radar fire control systems, respectively.[4] The K- and M-model conversions were typified by a pinched-looking black radome mounted in place of the J-model's Plexiglas nose cap, while retaining the rest of the J-style nose glazing. Some of the TB-25Ks were supplied to Air National Guard units as fire-control radar trainers.

Former B-25D (43-3797) became Royal Canadian Air Force (RCAF) Mitchell HD326 of 5 Operational Training Unit, photographed after World War Two, with new maple leaf insignia. Aircraft received modifications including bay-window waist enclosures and high doghouse tail emplacement similar (but not identical) to that built into H- and J-models at the factory. (Peter M. Bowers collection)

B-25s continued to serve foreign air forces after World War Two. Canada and the Netherlands, both wartime Mitchell users, operated B-25s in the postwar era. While Canadian B-25s were used in training and miscellaneous roles after the end of World War Two, some Dutch Mitchells in southeast Asia saw later combat. A Netherlands East Indies Air Force B-25 (ex-USAAF 43-28184) was downed by Indonesians at Kalibanteng early in August 1946, and another Dutch B-25 (Netherlands East Indies Air Force number 252; ex-USAAF 44-30507) was shot down at Palembang on 21

(Above) B-25 fire bombers in Arizona circa 1960 used bulging retardant tanks in their bomb bays. When B-25s fell out of favor as fire bombers in the United States, many languished until resurrected for the movie Catch-22 in the late 1960s. (Ken Shake)

Part of the fleet of Mitchells refurbished by Frank Tallman's Tallmantz Aviation for filming Catch-22 reposed at Orange County Airport, California, after filming in 1969. (Kenneth G. Johnsen)

NORTH AMERICAN B-25 MITCHELL

Used as a fire training hulk into the 1970s, this B-25J fuselage still carried quilted insulation between exposed fuselage frames. (Frederick A. Johnsen)

July 1947 as the Netherlands East Indies was embroiled in fighting between the Dutch and Indonesian nationals that ultimately saw the creation of an independent Indonesia. The resulting Indonesian Air Force did absorb three B-25s into its roster.[5]

Side view at Edwards Air Force Base in the 1950s shows long candy-striped data boom on left wingtip of a Mitchell used to teach test pilot school students how to perform flight tests. Yellow and red tail, wing, and fuselage panels helped identify this aircraft to other traffic. Postwar semi-collector-ring exhaust modification is evident, with a stack visible midway up the cowling. In the absence of a top turret, slope of the top of the fuselage is pronounced. Even though used as an unarmed training aircraft, this B-25 still retained cockpit side armor plate when photographed. (USAF)

Central and South American air forces got Mitchells from the United States. Brazil began receiving B-25s during World War Two; NAA engineer and author Norm Avery noted seven B-25Bs (40-2245, 2255, 2263, 2306, 2309, 2310, and 2316) were delivered to Brazil before December 1941.

Deliveries of Mitchells, including a number of J-models, to Brazil eventually exceeded 80 aircraft. Chile was allocated a dozen B-25Js in 1947; Peru received eight J-models that year. Venezuela operated a number of B-25s after World War Two. Colombia received three B-25Js in 1947; Uruguay operated about 10 Mitchells beginning in 1950. Mexico took delivery of three B-25Js in 1945, and pre-Castro Cuba bought four Mitchells in 1947; two more B-25s were confiscated by Cuba in 1947 as part of an aborted invasion.[6]

Nationalist Chinese air force crews operated more than 100 B-25s during and after World War Two; some were left behind to communist Chinese forces when the Nationalists moved to Formosa.

The same features that endeared the B-25 to the postwar U.S. Air Force for miscellaneous duties argue for the likelihood that at least some of the more than 800 B-25s received by the USSR during World War Two remained in some form of service into the postwar era.

Mitchells entered civilian service in the United States as executive aircraft, cargo haulers, camera platforms, and fire bombers.

[1] "Hayes Aircraft Finds: USAF Conversions Mean Big Business," *Aviation Week and Space Technology* magazine, 5 March 1956, Pp. 62-63. [2] N.L. Avery, *B-25 Mitchell — The Magnificent Medium*, Phalanx Publishing, St. Paul, Minnesota, 1992. [3] Interview, author with Norm L. Avery, 8 Jul 1997. [4] Peter M. Bowers and Gordon Swanborough, *United States Military Aircraft Since 1908*, Putnam, London, 1971. [5] N.L. Avery, *B-25 Mitchell — The Magnificent Medium*, Phalanx Publishing, St. Paul, Minnesota, 1992. [6] *Ibid*.

THE HEART OF THE MATTER

CARE AND FEEDING OF THE B-25

Following the use of 1,100 horsepower Pratt and Whitney R-1830-56C3-G engines in the predecessor NA-40, the B-25 entered a lifelong association with variants of the Wright R-2600 motor, a 14-cylinder, twin-row radial that, in typical production Mitchells, gave 1,700 horsepower per engine for takeoff.

In an ironic, albeit circumstantial, tribute to the B-25 engine package, civilian operators of many surplus PB4Y-2 Privateer fire bombers replaced the Privateer's Pratt and Whitney R-1830-94 engines (rated at 1,350 horsepower) with complete R-2600s in B-25 cowling, replacing the Privateer's characteristic oval cowling with round Mitchell sheetmetal and semi-collector exhaust system. A potentially life-saving arithmetic was at work in the conversion; at 1,700 horsepower apiece, four R-2600s on a big Privateer provide a total of 1,000 additional horsepower if called upon in an emergency. However, the so-called Super Privateers were officially redlined at the same power settings as their Pratt and Whitney-engined counterparts since that is what the airframe had been designed for.

Wright R-2600 radial engines powered B-25s like this B-25C-25-NA, fitted with individual exhaust stacks with their ports faired in cowling outlets. A North American Aviation technical summary refers to the stacks as

CRANK UP THE MITCHELL

Engine starting in a B-25 began with the master ignition switch on, and first the right booster pump on. The Dash-1 flight manual for the TB-25M instructed pilots to energize and mesh the starter switch, energizing for 10 seconds if on external power and 20 seconds if using the B-25's batteries. During this portion of the start-up sequence, the engine should tick over, turning at least four blades of the propeller to ensure liquid-lock was not a problem in the engine. The manual advised: "Discontinue starting if there is evidence of propeller balk or stall as damage to the engine may result from a liquid lock." With the right ignition switch indicating both right magnetos on, the right primer switch was used. According to the manual: "When the engine fires, continue to prime and stabilize rpm to between 800 and 1000 by throttle adjustment." Pilots were warned against excessive priming since the flow of gasoline would "dilute the oil on the cylinder walls and result in scoring of the walls... Excessive priming can create a fire hazard." After the engine fired, the mixture lever was to be moved to Full Rich position; "when a drop in RPM is noted, discontinue priming." The primer switch was then turned off, and the throttle set at 1200 rpm before repeating the sequence with the left engine.[1]

"Clayton-type flame-damping individual stacks." In later years, a semi-collector ring often replaced the upper stacks with a side-mounted exhaust, while the lower individual stacks remained in use. (NAA)

Ongoing tribute to the B-25's R-2600 engine package are the re-engined PB4Y-2 Privateers flown as fire bombers by Hawkins and Powers Aviation out of Grey Bull, Wyoming. Photographed at Lancaster, California, during the fire season of 1997, this "Super Privateer" uses the equivalent of two Mitchells' worth of Wright engines with semi-collector exhaust and high carburetor inlet atop cowling. Proximity of Privateer's wing leading edge to the collector exhaust stack results in heavy smudging on the wing. (Frederick A. Johnsen)

B-25 Takeoff

To a novice B-25 student pilot whose previous multi-engine experience was probably in smaller tail-wheeled trainers, the no-nonsense Mitchell might at first appear daunting. The flight manual says: "Takeoff in this aircraft varies from that of aircraft with a tail wheel during initial part of ground run only; the principal difference being in the angle of attack. In this aircraft, you start from a negative angle of attack and obtain a positive angle by raising the nose wheel. Plan your take-off according to the following variables affecting take-off technique: gross weight, wind, type of runway, and height and distance of the nearest obstacles."[2]

For a normal takeoff, not complicated by crosswinds or a short runway, the flight manual for the TB-25M said:

"1. Roll into take-off position, align the aircraft with the runway and neutralize the control column.

2. Advance throttles slowly, using them to obtain initial directional control. As soon as the aircraft is rolling straight, equalize the throttles and advance them smoothly and steadily to take-off power.

3. Check engine instruments for readings within normal operating range.

4. During take-off run, maintain directional control with rudders and throttles. Brakes should not be used unless absolutely necessary.

5. If an engine fails before go-no-go speed is reached, the aircraft can be stopped in the remaining runway distance. If failure occurs above go-no-go speed, take-off must be continued with one engine.

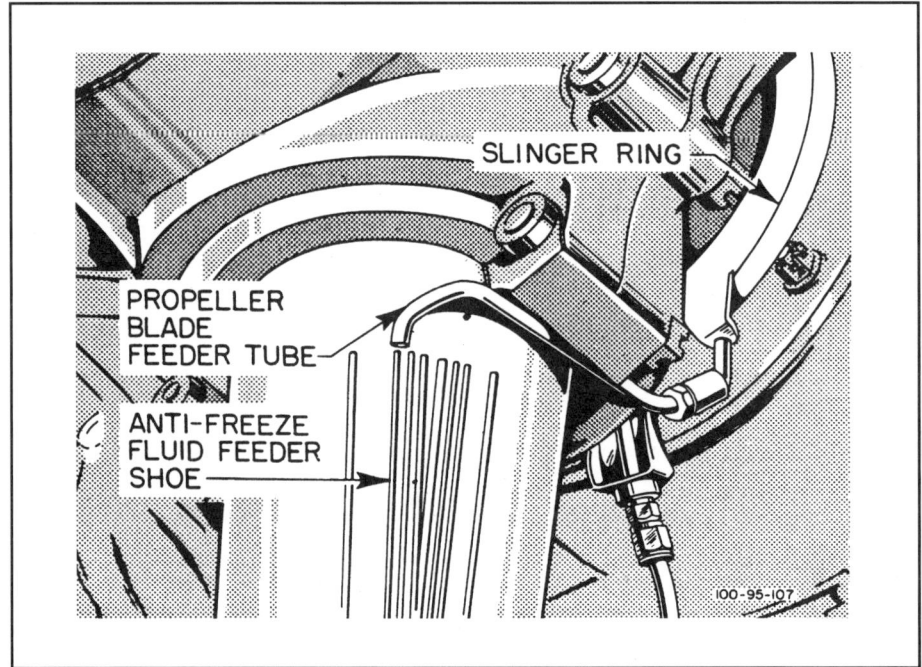

Detail drawing shows B-25 Hamilton-Standard propeller anti-icing devices. Bent feeder tube delivers fluid to grooved "shoe" to disperse it along the blade as it whirls in flight. (Courtesy Fred LePage)

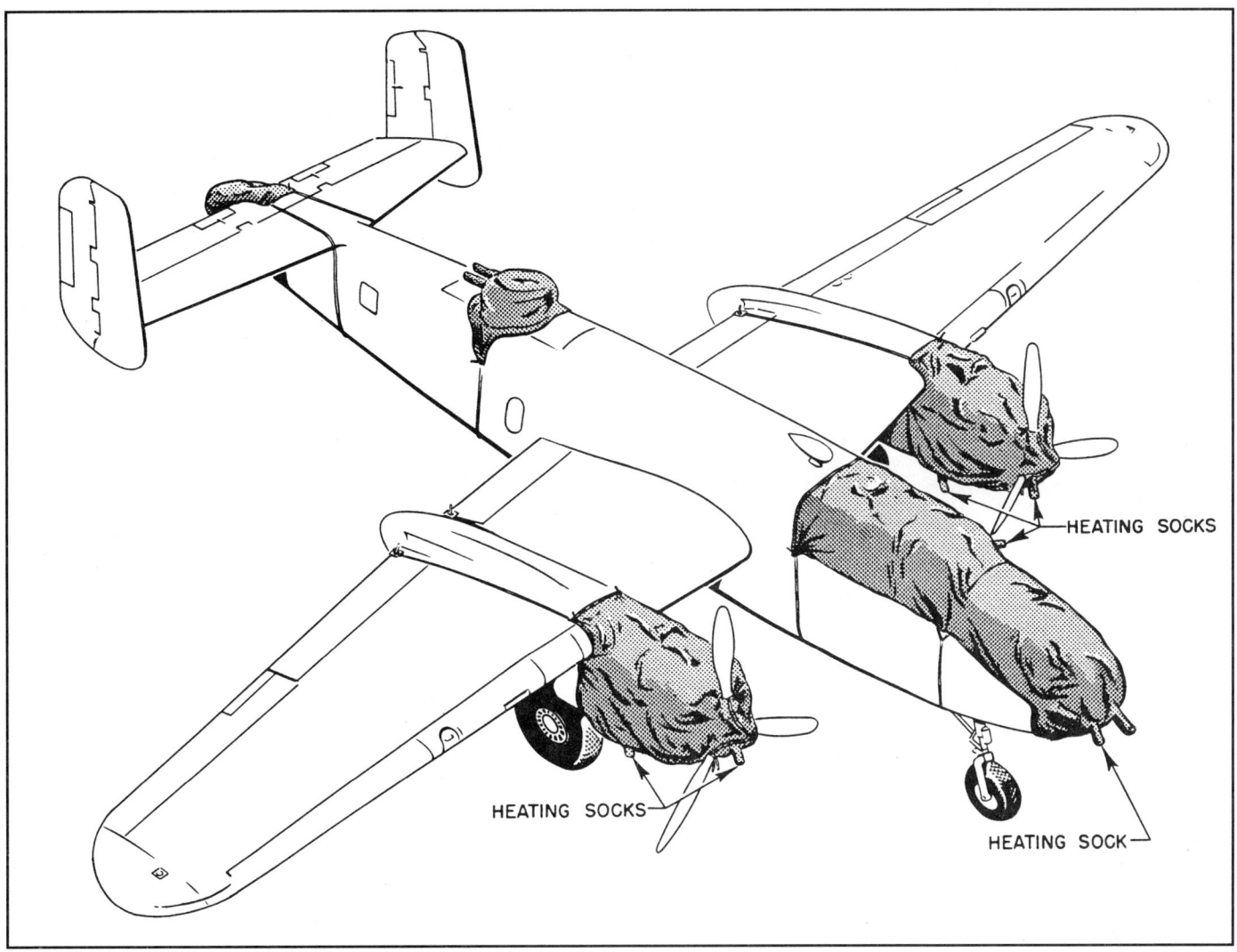

Protective covers on a B-25D show heating sock inlets where ground heat ducts can be introduced to warm specific parts of the aircraft. (Courtesy Fred LePage)

6. At approximately 75-85 MPH IAS (Indicated Airspeed), lift nosewheel slightly; then as speed increases, allow aircraft to fly itself off.

7. Normal take-off speed for gross weight of 26,000 pounds is 110-120 MPH IAS."[3]

COLD WEATHER OPERATIONS

There's a difference between flying an aircraft from a temperate climate into cold upper air, and back to moderate temperatures, and in operating for prolonged periods in a frigid environment where natural warmth is missing. Cold-soaking, a phenomenon by which an aircraft's systems become cold round the clock, can lead to balky performance not encountered in an aircraft that merely passes through cold temperatures briefly during a mission.

The B-25 Mitchell was in service around the world, including Alaska, where cold-soaking and other cold-weather ambushes awaited. Some B-25s were winterized with modifications intended to meet the challenge of a freezing environment. If cold weather threatened to congeal engine oil, an oil dilution system for each engine, as described in a B-25D and H-model winterization manual, "withdraws engine fuel from a fitting at the fuel inlet to the carburetor and introduces it into the oil system at the oil Y drain fitting, where it mixes with the oil. This action lowers the viscosity of the oil and facilitates easier engine starting in cold weather."[4]

To keep ice from clinging to propeller blades, some B-25s had Hamilton-Standard props with anti-icer fluid delivery systems. This system depended on a 10-gallon tank

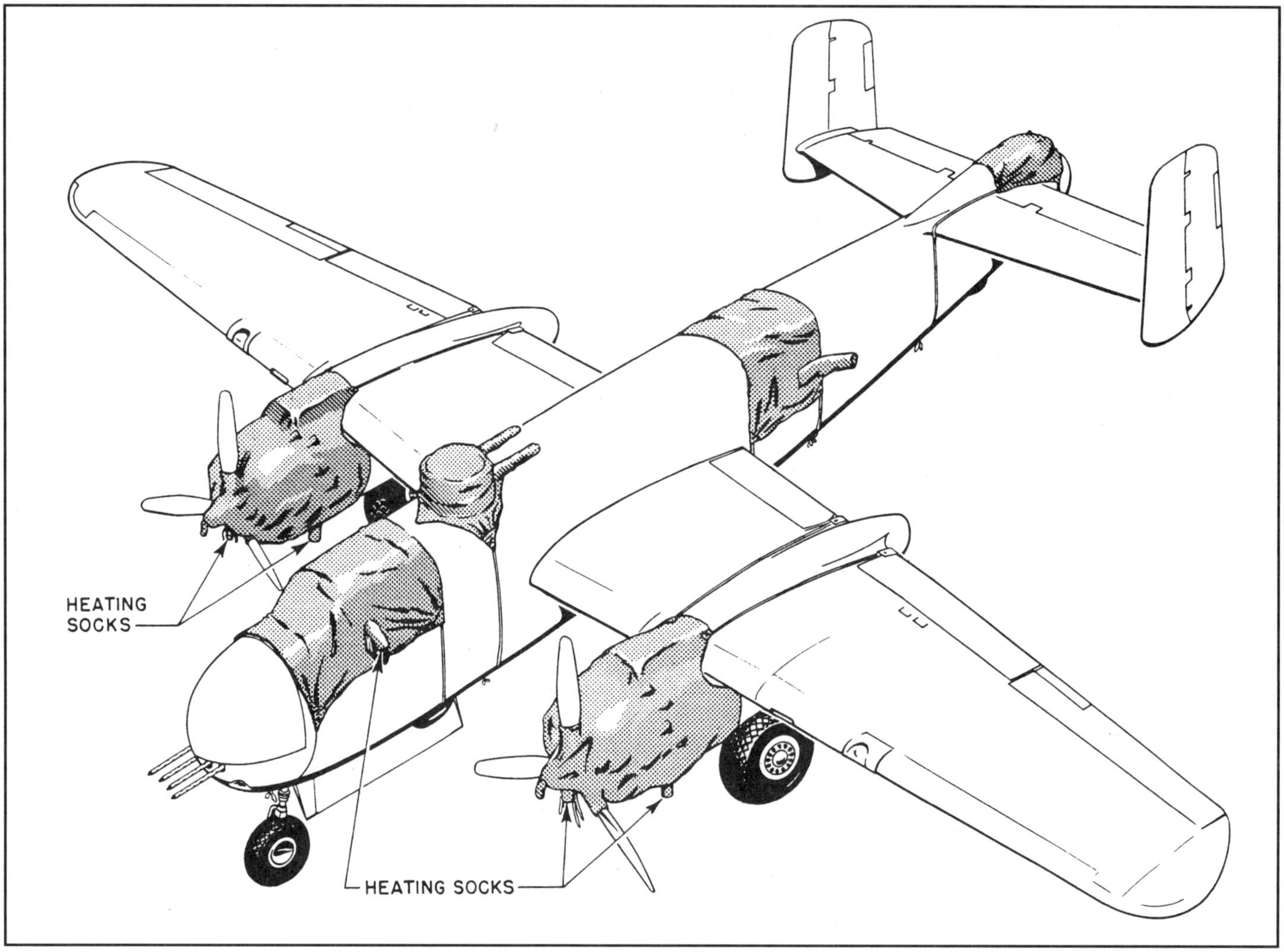

B-25H added waist section protective cover; heating sock beside pilot's cockpit allowed warm air to be introduced inside flight deck while aircraft was parked. In flight, warm air in the H-model's heating ducts kept the nose guns within operating temperature range. (Courtesy Fred LePage)

of anti-freeze solution mounted in the right engine nacelle, with a pump and lines feeding both propellers. As described in the NAA winterization text: "The pump delivers the fluid to the slinger ring mounted on the propeller through a feeder tube located on the front of each engine. From the slinger ring, the fluid, impelled by centrifugal force, flows into the feeder tube on each propeller blade and then onto the leading edge of the blade." Grooved propeller blade feed shoes assured satisfactory distribution of the fluid. The manual noted: "These shoes will be installed at the discretion of the Air Service Command when the airplane is assigned to cold weather operation."[5]

Available for main landing wheels on B-25s assigned to cold climates were snow and ice tires, specially fitted with metal cleats to enhance traction on snow or ice. Winterized B-25s were to have J-1 gun heaters installed on the cover plates of each .50-caliber weapon. A clear-view window panel on the pilot's side in B-25Hs and on both sides in B-25Ds could be "opened while flying in snow, rain, or sleet to ensure the pilot of better vision."[6]

In an effort to aid crews, all B-25 equipment that was satisfactory for use under cold weather conditions was to be marked with a yellow dot. To avoid formation of ice in the gasoline system of the B-25, Mitchells in cold climates were to have all fuel tank and fuel system drains opened to eliminate water in the system "immediately prior to removing the airplane from a heated hangar to outside cold temperatures," the winterization guide said.[7]

A 250-watt, 115-volt electric heater

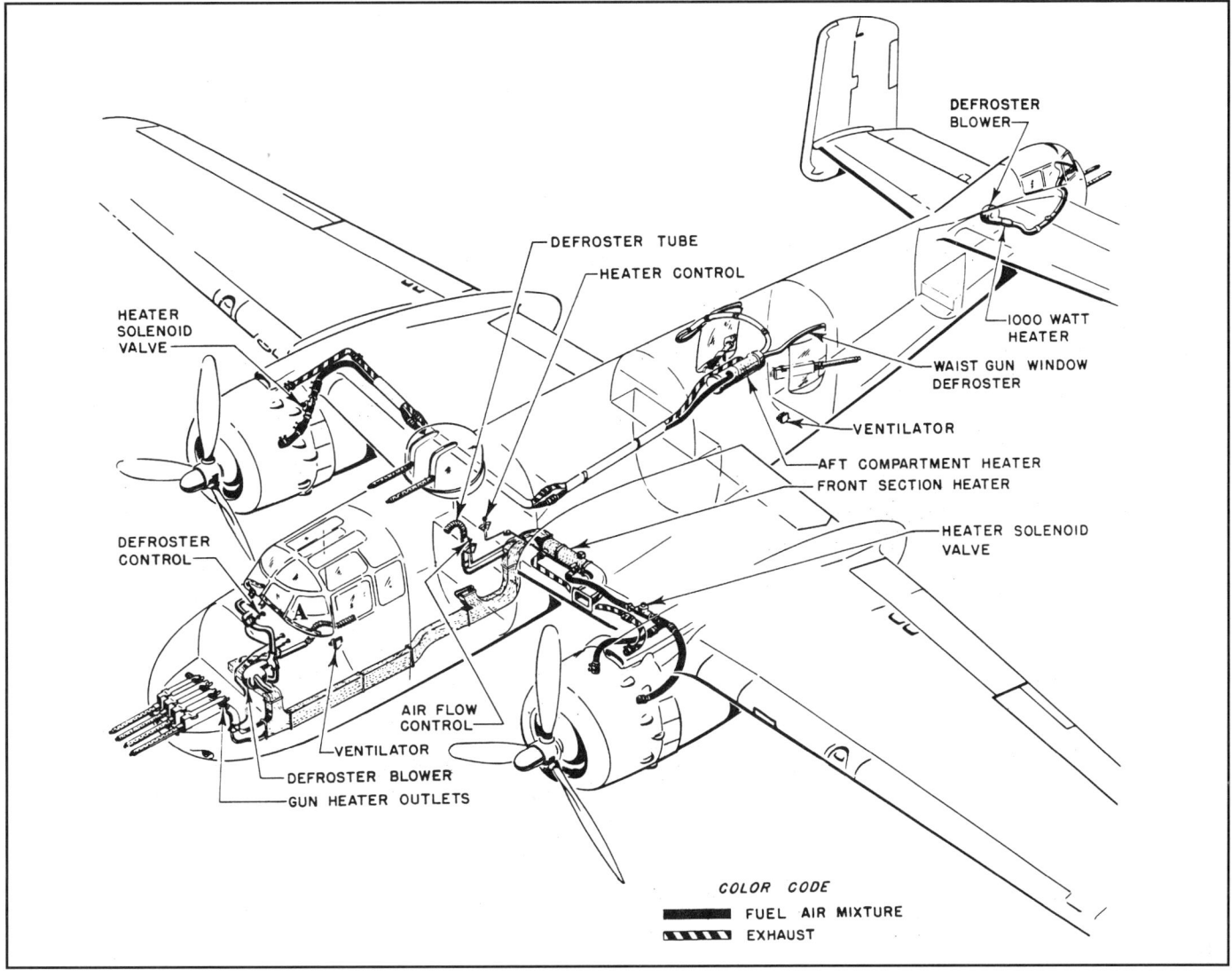

Heater in left wing of B-25H-1 warmed forward portions of this Mitchell including nose gun bay; another heater near the waist kept the aft compartment warm in flight. The combustion heaters ran on a fuel-air mixture. (Courtesy Fred LePage)

described in the B-25D and H-model winterization guide had an immersible element that could be inserted into the Mitchell's oil tank. The heater was to be inserted as soon as possible after engine shutdown, and left in place until the engine was to be started again. If the heater was not used continuously, "three to five hours of operation of the heater will be required before the oil will be sufficiently warm to start the engine." Arctic operations required a much higher level of aircraft attention and servicing between flights to forestall the effects of cold-soaking.[8]

Mitchell crews were advised to park their bombers on insulated material instead of directly on snow or ice, " to prevent the tires from freezing to the surface. Lack of such precautions frequently results in the tearing off of large chunks of rubber when the airplane is again moved."

If inadequate mooring was available for the B-25, crews were instructed to dig holes about eight inches deep and eight inches across into the frozen ground. Two notched stakes were to be placed "crosswise in each hole and then tie the mooring ropes to the stakes. Fill the holes with water, which will freeze and hold the stakes and rope fast." Ingenuity was paramount.[9]

[1] *Flight Handbook - USAF Series TB-25M Aircraft*, T.O. 1B-25(T)M-1, 15 Apr 57. [2] *Ibid.* [3] *Ibid.* [4] *Winterization of B-25D and B-25H Series Airplanes for 1943-44*, North American Aviation, Inc., Report No. NA-5792, North American Aviation, Inglewood, Calif., 15 Aug 43. [5] *Ibid.* [6] *Ibid.* [7] *Ibid.* [8] *Ibid.* [9] *Ibid.*

Significant Dates

Key Dates in the History of the B-25 Mitchell

January 1939
First flight of NAA-developed NA-40-1 bomber design that metamorphosed into the B-25.

5 September 1939
Contract date for procurement of 184 B-25s, B-25As, and B-25Bs.

19 August 1940
First flight of B-25 (40-2165) made by Vance Breese.

25 February 1941
First flight of B-25A (40-2189).

9 November 1941
Edward Virgin made first flight of B-25C (41-12434).

March 1942
B-25s became first U.S. bombers sent to the Soviet Union under Lend-Lease; eventually 870 Mitchells were furnished the Soviets.

18 April 1942
Sixteen B-25s under command of Lt. Col. Jimmy Doolittle launched from aircraft carrier USS *Hornet* and bomb targets in Japan, bringing the first bombing raid to the Japanese homeland. The raid improved morale in the United States, and caused the Japanese to rethink the disposition of their air defense assets.

14 January 1943
U.S. Navy ordered Mitchells, under designation PBJ, for the Marine Corps.

14 April 1943
Date of largest Mitchell contract, for 4,318 B-25Js.

4 November 1943
Chinese-American Composite Wing of 14th Air Force entered combat on this date with B-25s.

6 September 1944
Far East Air Forces (FEAF) B-25s attacked Buayan Airfield, thereby conducting the first USAAF medium bomber raid on the Philippines since early 1942.

15 November 1944
PBJ-1H successfully landed on and launched from aircraft carrier USS Shangri-La during tests in the Atlantic not far from Norfolk, Virginia.

January 1959
Last TB-25 in U.S. Air Force service as a trainer was retired at Reese Air Force Base, Texas.

21 May 1960
Retirement of the last converted staff transport B-25 from active Air Force inventory.

January 1969
Impressive fleet of 18 B-25s mustered by Frank Tallman began assembling in Mexico for filming of movie *Catch-22*.